These are actual testimonie at The40DayMiracle.com.

_____

This really does work. First of all I thank God for The 40 Day Miracle. I have seen results that I could not have imagined would have happened. The doors are being opened. I have gotten a new position that I applied for. All the other times I applied my supervisor blocked it. But this fast was in place and he could not stop or block it. My relationship is moving in a positive direction. My finances are being blessed. My child and his children are blessed. Our families are blessed. I thank God for this and will continue because I see that as I delight myself in God, He will give me the desires of my heart.

_____

Well, my 40 days are finished. There have been so many amazing things happening since I started the program, and I will do it all over again in 3 months. I do feel a new me and even my daughter is noticing it as well as others. The program has made me see where I falter and I am correcting them. I even laugh when I catch myself faltering because before I would not even have noticed or even paid attention to it.
I suggest The 40 Day Miracle to everyone I can. I am planting seeds. It is not important how many do the program, it's getting it out there and God is the One who will see if the seeds fall into fertile ground and make it grow.

_____

God is so good to me! Since I have been on The 40 Day Miracle, others have been praying for the return of my car, which was stolen on Dec. 03. I fasted and prayed for the return of my vehicle. Praise God, on Dec. 14, my car was located. God showered me with another blessing; the car was released to me and three days after my car was returned, I was offered a position with a company here in town. I was down to almost nothing in my checking account. When I checked my account this evening, I discovered that I had an increase in my amount from the unemployment! I started praising God. When all things seem impossible and there seems to be no way out, God is on time, in time of need! I have been truly blessed while on The 40 Day Miracle!

———————————

I am beginning day 3 and already am feeling great! It is such a challenge to think about who I'm going to compliment, who am I going to give something to today, and really feeling a partnership with God! I love myself for not overeating! I've enjoyed my Bible reading time too! I thank God for sending MountainWings.com into my life! I need and expect a miracle! I am 51 years old and am out of control with food, anger, greed, and envy. I want to be a better person and I believe God brought me to this. I am excited about it! Please pray for me!

———————————

When I started this program I knew my life needed a change. There was so much going on in my life; I think I had lost my focus. I am amazed at how much now, only on day two, my life has changed. I am excited about this 40-Day Miracle. I feel it is huge and is going to change lives all over the world. I have told everyone I come in contact with about the program plus sent e-mails. I can already feel my walk with God getting stronger. I look forward to my time with God and I'm enjoying my Bible study. It's like I have a new found peace in me and it's greater than before. I think maybe for the first time God has complete control. I'm on day two and already looking forward to my next 40 days after this. It's great to know there are people all over the world doing this with me. I will pray for all of you, and all of you please pray for me.

I just want to say how awesome God is. These 30 days have been a revealing period for me. I was dealing with "PEGLAGS" (7 deadly sins) that I wasn't even aware of!! In all things by prayer, supplication and thanksgiving to God, He is giving me a peace that surpasses all understanding. In light of my current unemployment, I should be anxious, but I have a peace that only Jesus can give. I'm so thankful to the Bronners for sharing these truths.

Since I started the 40-day Miracle 3 days ago, my life has changed. Although my son still has heart trouble, the 7 tests that were run on him ALL came back negative. Praise the Lord!!!! Even though he is still in pain and all, we are so much relieved.

Anger and gluttony are two areas that I have been in warfare with the enemy. I thank God that I had success in the area of anger today, and I made some progress in the area of food. I see myself getting stronger as I draw closer to the Lord during this 40-day period of purification.

Oh, My God...I had no idea that all of this stuff that's been buried deep inside of me would leave such an empty hole in my gut! But then again, what do I expect? The 40 Day Miracle is cleansing stuff from generational curses that extend farther than I can imagine. For the last two days I couldn't identify my feelings. At times I felt empty, lonely, bored to death, and other times I felt indecisive. Wow, this 40 Day Miracle has opened up "pandora's box" deep inside of me. What I realize is I have to allow myself to feel the feelings. I have tried to sedate with anything that fits into the realm of the 7 deadly sins, and I have to fill in that empty space using the tools in the Bible to finally be free or that old stuff will come right back. That's why I am putting so much into The 40 Day Miracle. I am tired of short changing God and cheating myself of all of my inheritance because I was afraid to fulfill my destiny.

I am thankful that the Bronner brothers allowed God to use them for this. How many people did God go to with this idea before someone was bold enough to step out and do it? I thank God that He still has servants who listen and do. Here I am at the end of my second week and if I come out of this with nothing but the fact that I am now spending 56 minutes a day with my Father I will be happy, but I am looking for the complete package. I would recommend this to anyone who is looking for a breakthrough in their life and who can commit to 40 days. You will never be the same after this 40-day consecration/fast, and it doesn't take the entire 40 days to see results. I saw results after 3 days and it just keeps getting better.

4

During this 40-Day Miracle I have undergone some training and I am becoming skilled in how to face the enemy. I understand who I am and Who lives in me! I am becoming adept at stepping aside and letting Christ face my opponent. Is anything too difficult for Me? Wow! You talk about strength. You talk about the battle already being won. I've learned how to let go and let God!

———————————

I started this pledge October 11. I went to the doctor yesterday and I was told that I had lost 5 pounds. Great news! I don't eat like I used to. It is so easy to push that plate away. If I overeat, I get cramps in my stomach. This has been a real challenge for me, but by the grace of God, I will make it to the 40th day. Good things are happening in my life. It has been tough and rough, but fulfilling. I will do it for the rest of my life. This was much needed in my life.

———————————

I just can't explain the excitement and joy that I feel going into The 40 Day Miracle.

———————————

The beginning hasn't been easy, but each day gets easier.

The 40 Day MIRACLE

120 Selig Dr.
Atlanta, GA 30336
www.40day.com

ISBN 0-9725818-2-0(paperback)

Writing, editing, and proofing services by holywriters.com
Leigh McMutry, Britte Blair, and Shelli Davis,
Art and layout by CrawfordAdvertising.com

The40DayMiracle.com

Are you ready for your Miracle?

Introduction

"This is going to be easy! I only have to do this for 40 days? Piece of cake!" These were the thoughts going through my head when I first accepted the challenge. As a matter of fact, I wasn't really looking for a miracle. I wanted to prove that I'm pretty close to perfect and that I live my life right 98% of the time (pride).

When I was asked to write about my experiences incorporating the sermons of the program, I thought, "BRING IT ON!!!" How hard could it really be to abstain from the seven deadly sins? On the surface it seemed easy. Looking at myself in the mirror, on the outside, I look fine, no problems. I'm a good person, a phenomenal Christian and a great mother and wife. At least that's what I thought when I started.

I have three small children, all under the age of 8. I began brushing their teeth for them when they each turned two. One at a time I began training them on how to properly brush their teeth in the morning and at night explaining to them the importance of brushing. Their teeth were so white that they were often complimented on how clean and pretty their teeth were. Adults would even ask me if I was using some kind of whitening system (don't ask). Anyway, because their teeth were white on the surface, I was confident that I was doing a great job and that certainly when the expert, the dentist, took a look, he would be impressed.

I made their first dentist appointment when the oldest was five and I was excited. I was so proud and thrilled and confident that I woke up early that morning and cooked an extra special breakfast. The kids got dressed and then we did what we always do...we brushed our teeth ...together. While they were rinsing their brushes, I was flossing my teeth and rinsing my mouth with mouthwash...just like I always do.

We finally got in the truck and drove to the dentist's office. The first thing the receptionist said was, "Wow, look at all of those beautiful teeth! They are so white and pretty." Of course, you know exactly what I was thinking. I was so proud that I wanted to go to the back room with the dentist just so I could hear all of the wonderful comments, but no such luck. I had to stay in the waiting area. There I sat, imagining how wonderful things were going and about how I was going to take the kids out for lunch and maybe even for some ice cream, and at that moment after about an hour, the door opened.

The dental assistant asked my husband and me to come to the back office. She sat us down and showed us the children's x-rays and said, "I know they do a good job brushing because their teeth are white and clean, but they have cavities." CAVITIES???????? This nurse must be nuts, blind or the x-ray had some dirt on it. There's no way!!! She began to ask questions and dig deeper and I realized what I kind of already knew. Cavities are hidden, and they tend to creep up on you when you're not really paying attention. And worse than that, even when you are paying attention, they can creep up on you when you give up on your routine.

My point? That's how the seven deadly sins were in my life: invisible, silent, creeping up on me because I wasn't really paying attention. "I don't think I'm overweight; certainly I don't overeat," I thought. But sure enough, I would eat one serving of a meal, see if I'm full and then eat two or three more servings until I was full. It was gluttony...just one of the seven sins. You wouldn't be able to look at me to tell that I was guilty of being a glutton. One hour into The 40 Day Miracle and "BRING IT ON" turned into, "YIKES! What have I gotten myself into?" Most of these sins are subconscious sins. They are sins that we don't even realize we are committing; sins that require thought and effort to overcome.

Once I realized that I was neglecting to floss my children's teeth or to allow them to use a kid safe fluoride to rinse their mouths, I did better. It wasn't easy to change. It takes a little bit more time to get everyone out of the bathroom now, it makes things a little messier now, and sometimes it seems the extra steps make the routine a little chaotic first thing in the morning; but it's well worth the extra time and chaos.

Likewise, once I started the program, it was hard to adjust. It took a lot more brainpower to remember that I was working toward a spiritual goal and purpose. I was no longer comfortable. I couldn't just interact with people anymore; I had to be conscious and mindful of what I was saying and thinking. I even had to be mindful of using the word "I." But the miracle of spiritual freedom and understanding are well worth the challenge. And now that I know better, I do better and I can see those once invisible sins before they have a chance to sneak up on me.

I am confident that after you read this book, you will have the strength, power, and confidence to complete the 40-day challenge of abstaining from the 7 deadly sins. And after your 40 days, I am confident that you will receive a miracle and a new life with new relationships. This program was created by God but manifested through three brothers whom I have great admiration and respect for. Individually, they are pastors Nathaniel H. Bronner, Jr., C. Elijah Bronner and James Bronner, but together they are known as Brothers of the Word (BOTW). In this book, you will first learn what you will need to get started and what you must do on a daily basis. You will also read written versions of their sermons explaining each of the sins in detail and how to overcome them. Once you've started the program, you will start to see a change in yourself and the people around you. You've heard it a million times, but seriously, welcome to the beginning of the rest of "Your Life."

Chapter One

Getting Started

————•◦◦•————

You did it! You actually made it to Chapter One. You may laugh, but there will be many people stricken with "sloth" (another deadly sin) who won't even make it beyond the title page. The fact that you've gotten this far shows that you have a desire to be different and to live differently. It shows that you understand that this is something you need to do and you're willing to try. I

promise you won't regret reading this book or starting this program. As a matter of fact, if you're like me, you'll wonder what took you so long. However, before you read any further, I must be honest. Yes, this program is everything it claims to be. Yes, it will work. Yes, you will receive a miracle at the end of your forty days, but NO, it won't be easy. That's why you have this book and me to take along with you. Well, not "me" physically, but "me" in words and thoughts. I'll be cheering you on along the way. And since we're all being honest here, I might as well tell you that I tried to start the program without a day of prayer and preparation and let's just say, I had to start over.

A day of prayer and preparation is not a requirement, but for me, it was VERY necessary. Before starting my first day, I mean, before starting my second first day, I decided to take a day to pray to God for the strength to start and for the strength to endure. Things that would normally end up on my prayer list were put aside for another day so that I could concentrate totally on this life mission. I also took time to read and understand the foundation of The 40 Day Miracle as outlined by the BOTW using Biblical teachings and principles. The program can be started without a preparation day, but having a COMPLETE understanding of what you will go through will help you to endure. It will be difficult to see yourself completing the program without understanding.

I'm sure by now you're aware that The 40 Day Miracle is a mission in which you have decided to abstain from the seven deadly sins for 40 days. If you didn't know that before now then either I haven't done a very good job or you were daydreaming through the first couple of pages, which means you need to start over. Okay, now that we're all on the same page, what are the seven deadly sins? The seven deadly sins are the seven sins that the church decided hundreds of years ago were the most detrimental sins to man. Basically all of the "spiritual degradation" that we have in the world can be narrowed down to these seven deadly sins: Pride, Envy, Greed, Lust, Sloth, Anger, and Gluttony.

"Why 40 days?" I asked the same thing. I mean, why not 7 days? I've always thought of seven as the number of "completion," besides if I do it in seven days then that's one day per sin. It also means I don't have to "go through" for very long. Well, I'm glad you asked. "Forty is the Biblical number of major change and preparation for destiny." The seven days were a great argument, but it takes all 40 days...that's only 5.7 weeks if you were calculating. Seriously though, the 40 days can be referenced in the Bible. Take a look:

- To prepare for the new world it rained for **40 days and 40 nights**
- After the rain stopped, Noah waited **40 days** to open the Ark window
- Embalming required **40 days**
- Moses stayed on the mountain **40 days** (TWICE); his face shone afterwards
- The spies spent **40 days** searching out the Promised Land
- Israelites spent **40 years** in the wilderness before reaching the Promised Land
- Goliath challenged for **40 days** before being killed by David
- Elijah, strengthened by one angelic meal, went **40 days** to Mt. Horeb
- Jonah warned Nineveh they had **40 days** before God overthrew the city
- Jesus fasted and was tempted **40 days** in the wilderness
- Jesus was seen on the earth **40 days** after His crucifixion

As you can see, often when God wanted to prepare someone for a truly great destiny, He took 40 days and sent them through an experience somewhat unpleasant to the flesh. This experience will wear on you and will have many points of discomfort for you, but hold on, your miracle is at the end.

BOTW say that to start the program, you need **3D Vision**. Not 3D Glasses, 3D Vision. Please do not think that images will pop out of this book at you. 3D Vision means that in order to "see" yourself complete this program, you must **Discover,**

Decide, and **Do**. *Discovering* simply means understanding the significance of the 40 days and the seven deadly sins, all of which you can learn with this book. *Deciding* means to make up your mind to do this. Since you're reading Chapter One, that means you've made up your mind to do this. And finally, you must do. *Doing* means reading this book and the daily proclamation; discovering and deciding are not enough. You have to actually follow the instructions outlined in the program and make the sacrifice.

In the back of this book is a copy of the Daily Proclamation. The Daily Proclamation is the backbone of the program. You must read it twice a day and follow the guidelines and promises that are outlined. As you will see, the Proclamation must be read out loud. Silent reading is not an option. Reading the proclamation twice a day really tugs at your spirit and is a very helpful reminder of what you're doing. It doesn't make the sacrifices easy, but it does help to keep you focused.

The Proclamation and other helpful tools including the audible versions of the sermons in their entirety can also be found on 40day.com. If for whatever reason you are unable to get a computer, CD player or cassette player to listen to the sermons, the sermons are outlined in the following chapters and can be read in place of listening to the sermons. Before continuing, turn to the back of the book and read the Proclamation and then come right back. I'll hold your place for you until you return.

Welcome Back!

I'm glad you came back! What did you think? Starting to see parts of your life that need to change? "Need" is the key word. I can't say it enough; this is something that we all desperately NEED to do. You will have a better life.

Well, the sermons are about to start. You will begin hearing sermons from the Brothers of the Word. Although you will not be able to hear them audibly, you will be able to hear them spiritually as you read. I will be with you as you read. I will be cheering you on as you challenge life as you know it. I'll be at the end of the sermons in the "It's Me" section and I will remind you of the Proclamation as it relates to each sermon. You can do this! You need to do this! You will be 40 days older in 40 days. What will your life be like on that day? Will you be the same?

Chapter Two

Pride: Stiff Necked Saints

By Nathaniel H. Bronner, Jr.

For those of you reading this book, I thank you and welcome. I am excited about The 40 Day Miracle because it is so life-changing. If at any point you are unable to read or maybe you're working on something else, please feel free to listen to the sermons in their entirety on 40day.com. In this chapter, I am going to be dealing with the first of the 7-part series dealing with the 40-day miracle. It will become one of the most valuable things that you will ever possess and ever experience.

This chapter's message is about pride. In Deuteronomy 31:27, the Bible says, "For I know thy rebellion and thy stiff neck. Behold while I am yet alive with you this day ye have been rebellious against the Lord and how much more after my death." The leader was saying, if while I'm living, you're stiff necked, stuck up, and rebellious then I know once I die you're going to get even worse. Stiff Necked Saints (SNS) are nothing new; even the chosen of Israel were SNS. These were the chosen "sainted" ones and they were stiff necked. As sad as it may sound, we still have a lot of stiff necks in the church. I'm not talking about those in the world; I'm talking about Christians. We have a lot of proud, stuck up and stiff necked saints. Some of you just need to get your neck a little more limber. Think about it…sometimes when you're under a lot of stress and you decide to go to the massage therapist, where is the first place that they will massage? It's your neck. Why? Because it's stiff.

Pride from a spiritual standpoint is defined as the excessive belief in one's own abilities that interferes with the individual's recognition of the grace of God. When the church defined and enumerated the seven deadly sins, pride was always listed as number one. The church also refers to pride as the "granddaddy of all sins." It's the main one. It's the deadliest of the seven, but it's one that you often can see the least. It's a silent killer. Do you know even in the natural, in our physical body, the diseases that kill most of us are silent killers? High blood pressure, one of the leading diseases, is a silent killer. Cancer is the other big

killer; you don't know anything's wrong until you're almost dead. They are silent killers. So just as in the natural, in the spiritual, the thing that kills so many Christians and their spiritual lives is the silent killer of pride.

Even when you look at the word pride, in the middle of the word pride is 'I,' PRIDE. When you look at the word sin, in the middle of the word SIN is 'I.' Go ahead and say to yourself, "The problem with me is 'I.'" Once you recognize that the problem is 'I,' you can deal with it. It's because of the 'I' factor that gets so many of us in trouble and so many of us turn away from God because we think it's all about us and it's all about 'I.'

There once was this great athlete on a basketball team and he just thought he was the star of the team and everything revolved around him. His pride was so bad that it began to affect the attitude of those around him especially his fellow teammates so the coach decided to talk to him one day. The coach told him, "Don't you understand that there's no 'I' in TEAM?" The coach reminded him that he would have to become more of a team player. The young man responded, "Yes, I know there's no 'I' in team but there's no 'we' in TEAM either." The coach in essence was giving the young man a choice; either he could change or the team would change their starting line up. Are you willing to change?

The original sin was a result of pride. Adam and Eve wanted to be God. In Genesis 3:4-5, the serpent said unto the woman, "Ye should not surely die for God knows that in the day that you eat thereof, then your eyes shall be open and ye shall be gods knowing good and evil." That's how the devil got himself into a mess. He had a problem with pride. The devil got himself into a mess and then decided to bring Adam and Eve down with him using the persuasion of pride. In Isaiah, Chapter 14, beginning at verse 12, Isaiah is talking about the devil and questions, "How art thou fallen from heaven o Lucifer son of the morning? How are thou cut down to the ground

which did weaken the nations for thou has said in thine heart -
I will ascend into heaven; I will exalt my throne above the stars
of God; I will sit also upon the mount of the congregation on the
sides of the north; I will ascend above the heights of the crowds;
I will be like the most high." Basically what got Lucifer in
trouble was that he said I am going to take the place of God.
That's fundamentally what pride does. Pride in essence says I
will take the place of God.

Even in the Bible, in Proverbs, Chapter 6 beginning at verse
16, it says, "these six things doth the Lord hate, and seven are
an abomination unto Him." The first one is a proud look.
Basically, that's a stiff neck. A proud look refers to the way a
person looks, walks, acts, talks...there's just an air of pride
around them. That's the first thing that God named of the 7
things He hated, a proud look. Because we feel that it is all
about 'I' ("I am this" or "I've done this" and "I can do this" and
"This is mine" and "Do you know who I am?") we get it twisted
up about who's really in charge.

Even in ministry, in I Timothy 3:6, it says, when describing
the qualities of a bishop or an elder or an overseer, it clearly says
"not a novice lest being lifted up with pride he falls into the
condemnation of the devil." He said don't get a new man to
oversee anybody because it is so easy for him to get puffed up
because of pride. When you're put into an important position
over other people, especially when you're receiving praise, it's
very difficult to stay humble. It's not long before you start
believing, even as a pastor, "Look what I have done." Preachers
often say, "You know I built this ministry, and these members are
here because of me, and if I couldn't preach so well they
wouldn't be here. I've got an anointing that's so powerful that
when I lay hands on folks they fall. I even have the gift of

prophecy and the word of knowledge. I can sing so well and you haven't seen anyone do the holy dance until you've seen me do it." So it's not long before even preachers get lifted up in pride. If pride was able to get the best of an angel, and even the best of the chief angel, then don't you think we are sure targets?

There are four major things that cause us to be proud, and there are some reasonable things that you can do to deal with it. I can tell you right now that it's not easy. I have a problem with pride. Yes, I am a pastor, and I admit, I have a problem with pride. Pride is something you can feel within yourself and you can feel it in other people when you are around them. God spoke to me years ago and said that someday I would have the power to raise the dead. Me? I was sure of what He said. I just wasn't sure if He meant literally raising the dead at the funeral home or whether He just meant people whose spirits were dead. I just don't know. But the other thing I do know is that He said that with the power comes a problem. God said the problem would be my pride. He said my pride wouldn't be able to handle the power.

I was sitting there thinking about it. Now what if God was really talking about raising the dead out of the funeral home? Do you know what would happen if I had the power to raise the dead out of the funeral home? There aren't many preachers raising people from the dead these days; as a matter of fact, I don't really know of any. So imagine what fame and recognition would come to me if I had the power to raise the dead. I would only have to raise about 2 or 3 dead people and I would instantly become known as the preacher who has the power to raise the dead. Imagine the wealth and notoriety. People wouldn't see God, they would see me. That's usually what happens. When God does something great, people don't see a powerful God, they see a powerful man. When God does something great in your life, who do you see, Him or you?

In the world of being a preacher, people are often trying to get to me. They believe that if they can just touch me then maybe some anointing might rub off of me onto them. Beliefs such as these are usually how a preacher ends up on a "pedestal." And God, knowing that such power would lift me up instead of Him said, "Your pride can't handle it." It's true, God knows me. And I say to you, God knows you.

We always wonder why we didn't receive certain blessings or gifts; well, it's because God already knows that your pride won't allow you to handle some of the gifts, talents and blessings that He wants to give to you. No matter what we may think, God knows us and there's some stuff we cannot handle. In other words, there are some things that we will accept without giving God praise or we will accept them and forget God. For some people it's a new car and for others it may be as simple as a new hat. Some people get a new hat and not only will they not talk to you - they won't let you talk to them. If you can't handle a new hat, you can forget the ability to raise the dead. Pride is real. What gift is your pride standing in the way of?

The first of the four major things that puffs us up are possessions and money. It doesn't really make a difference how much it is or what it is, possessions and money easily lift us up to the point of having a "proud look." It doesn't matter if it is that hat or a promotion or new house. Possessions and money puff us up. We can be one house payment ahead, have a cushion in the bank and a new car and we easily begin to forget God and think of ourselves only and those things that we did to get to that point in our lives. Possessions will change you. The question is how will you change and how will you handle the change?

I have a Mercedes, a Jeep and a BMW motorcycle. The Jeep is the only vehicle that I have that most people would consider "common" or easily attainable. However, when I go places in my S-series Mercedes and get out, people look at me a little differently. I honestly feel different in it. I'm stepping out of it onto the same ground, using my same two feet, but it doesn't feel the same. When I get out of the Jeep I just hop out; but when I get out of the Mercedes, some how I feel myself gliding out. I was at a red light not too long ago in my Mercedes and another driver pulled up beside me. The man rolled down the window and said, "that's a sharp car." That one comment just does something to you. He would have never said that had I been driving the Jeep.

When I drive the BMW motorcycle, no matter where I go, most people are in awe that BMW even makes motorcycles so they sit and stare for a moment. Sometimes I hear, "Man that's a sharp motorcycle; I didn't know BMW made motorcycles." Of course I feel differently; I feel important. I have something that is rare and leaves people in awe when they see it. I used to have a Honda motorcycle, but that's not as rare and so I ride the BMW differently. The BMW makes you sit differently. You just do.

So pride is real and no matter who you are, having "stuff" will affect you. Money and possessions make it real hard to stay humble. That's just the truth. The Bible says in Deuteronomy 8:10 that "When you have eaten and are satisfied, praise the Lord your God for the good land that He has given you. Be careful that you do not forget the Lord your God failing to observe His commands, His laws and His decrees that I am giving you this day. Otherwise, when you eat and are satisfied, when you build five houses and settle down and when your herds and flocks grow large and your silver and gold (that's money) increase and all you have is multiplied, then your heart will become proud and you will forget the Lord your God." In other words, if you don't stay before Him and keep His commandments, then when you are blessed and your possessions have multiplied, you will forget Him and will say that your success was obtained by the strength of your own hands. What a dangerous thing to believe.

First of all you can see it in the natural. Even in business you must have an analytical mind to look at things. When you start looking at it analytically, you may say things like, "I worked hard on this. I'm smarter than the competitor and that's why I got his business." We say our hands have produced greatly which is only a partial truth.

As my business began to prosper and grow, and as I could feel my family moving up in status, I looked at myself and I thought, "I'm pretty smart because my business is booming." It happens to all of us and we have to stop and think about it. If you think about your greatest success, you will be able to trace every link in the chain back to God. Just having the resources to even go into business for myself, I had to turn to God. I needed my daddy. I prayed that God would open doors, and He blessed me with my father and He blessed me with the means to borrow money. Who ordered my steps and placed those resources in front of me? I wouldn't have made it had God not shown favor.

Believe me, I know it was God because five of my business products that I have tried, have lost money and failed. God was showing me things that I could handle without pride getting in the way of my praise. One day, a prophet came to my office with an idea that I took up and it made money and paid all the bills from that point. Suppose God had not sent the prophet? We so easily forget how hard God was working behind the scenes. When we're down, we always remember God. As a matter of fact, we truly begin to "pray without ceasing." We've all prayed, "Lord, I'm yours. Lord, I submit myself unto thee. Whatever you want me to do, I'll do." But when we are full, if we haven't kept His commands, we are no longer telling Him, "Send me I'll go" because we feel we're already there.

As I had to look back over my own business and when I really looked at it, I was able to see the order of things. And yes, I was working hard, but I was working hard when all those things failed too. So why did one thing succeed over the others? It's because God wanted that for my life. You should always work hard, but just know, God is the catalyst and the reason for all of your success. Everything comes from God. When we use 'I' as an explanation for our success, pride enters in. That's why God says pride is an abomination and He hates it. Pride is the first and the "granddaddy" of the deadly sins.

The second thing that will boost pride is power. There is an old quote that simply states, "Absolute power corrupts absolutely." You see this in the Bible with the kings in story after story after story. Power is given to many different people in many different situations. For example, a man is considered "king" in his own home not because of riches but because of levels of authority. There are so many kinds of power that occur. You could have political power or authority over people at your job or it could just be your charismatic personality that gives you power. Believe me, charismatic power can travel very quickly to your head. So there are many kinds of power in many different arenas. The minute some people get power, they get very puffed up and very proud with a very stiff neck.

The third thing that makes us prideful is being pretty. The Bible even says in Ezekiel 28:17, "your heart became proud on the count of your beauty." Do you know it's hard to tell us something when we look good? When you are looking good, you spend more time in the mirror talking to yourself, smiling at yourself, practicing your walk or newest dance moves. I mean beauty can make us real proud. There's just no two ways about it. And please don't let us lose a little weight and get our hair done all in the same weekend. When we get in shape, get our hair looking good, get our face looking good, and put sharp clothes on, that stuff can puff you up like a balloon in a second. Lucifer was the most beautiful of all the angels and because he was so pretty and good-looking, he believed that he should be God.

The fourth thing that can really boost your pride is praise. How does it make you feel when someone gives you a compliment? If it's your hair, you sling it a little more. If it's your car, you go everywhere you can. If it's your walk, you don't mind parking away from the building. Our necks stiffen quickly when we get a compliment.

Some Sundays after service, my mother would come up to me and compliment me on the sermons; and I told her that as much as I love the praise, she had to stop complimenting me. My mother can really flower it up. She would come to me after church and say, "Oh boy, that message you preached was just awesome. It was just magnificent." Slowly but surely, I would just feel my neck begin to stiffen. I felt good, but I had to be honest with her. I said, "That's messing with my spirit." I was literally hanging on to every word; and with every word, I could feel pride rising in my spirit. I was trying to keep it under control because I knew that all this praise would mess me up.

You won't always be able to tell people not to compliment you and so that is why praise is real different. Praise belongs to God and it's up to you to make sure that's where it goes instead of letting it go to your head. Don't feel bad, most people can't handle praise and yet, one of the things dealing with The 40 Day Miracle is that you must compliment someone each day and watch their countenance change when you compliment them. It changes, but you have to be careful dealing with pride. Remember those four major things that boost pride: **(1) Possessions (Money), (2) Power, (3) Pretty (Beauty), and (4) Praise.**

Now how do we combat pride? First of all, you must recognize that you have a problem. That's VERY difficult to do because pride itself will convince you that you don't. So often, and it's a fact, pride wants you to believe that all is well and that you are not a "proud" person. So first thing you have to do is recognize that you have a problem even though your pride will try hard not to recognize it.

In Jeremiah 17:19, it says, "the heart is deceitful above all things." Your heart will tell you some serious stuff and sometimes that stuff is a serious lie. You begin thinking things like, "If God is over everybody, why am I the only one that's prospering? There must be something special about me because we've got the same God and look what He's done for me." The heart is deceitful above all things but first you have to recognize the truth. That's why when you read the daily proclamation, that first few paragraphs of the daily proclamation that you read every day deals with combating pride and that last sentence says, "I can do all things through Christ who strengthens me and I can do nothing successfully without God."

When you understand that it is by the power and divine orchestration of God and you begin to give God credit and praise for everything in your life, you can begin to fight pride. One good thing about me not taking credit for success is that it puts the responsibility back on God. If you are doing what God says, then you can handle anything because you will be in the Will of God. Now when I'm in charge it's a different thing. I am relieved when I can go somewhere and I'm not in charge. When I'm not in charge and something goes wrong, it's not my fault and I don't have to deal with it. Give it all to God, your failures and your successes, the complaints and the praise.

After you recognize and admit you have a problem with pride, then you must begin to fight it mentally. You can feel pride come up in you. You can feel your neck stiffen and your back straighten up. Everybody needs a certain degree of self-esteem, but you must be able to handle self-esteem without compromising your role as a child of God by believing that it's all up to you.

When you feel that spirit of pride come up in you, you have to fight. That's why Jesus said, "Hardly would a rich man enter into the kingdom of heaven." Of course I was a little concerned because I consider myself to be a rich man. So I have one of two choices: get poor or fight pride. Let me be honest, I don't want to become poor. I just don't want that at all. I've read that scripture many times and I make it a point not to criticize that rich young ruler. If you remember, the young ruler asked Jesus what should he do to get into Heaven and Jesus told him to give all of his stuff to the poor and come follow Him. No, Lord! I don't criticize that man because I don't know anybody who has attained a lot of riches who could honestly do that. The point is really not for us to give up all that we have, instead, the point is for us to give up those things that allow us to be proud.

Jesus knew that the young ruler couldn't handle a relationship with Him and wealth. Remember, we talked about what people can handle. If I had two weeks left to live, I could probably do it then; but for now, I choose to fight. I choose to fight to make sure that my possessions don't keep me from seeing God. You have to fight it mentally. I preached a sermon called, "How the Rich Get to Heaven" that explains in detail how to get to heaven if you are rich. You can listen to it at AirJesus.com.

One of the things that you have to know is that you must have the ability to control your pride. When you feel it rising up within your spirit, you have to be able to recognize it. You have to fight this feeling mentally and spiritually in order to decrease your pride and to become more humble. God talks about how He will exalt the humble but abase the proud.

In order to fight pride mentally, you must first seek the help of saints. James 5:16 says, "Confess your faults to one another and pray one for another that you may be healed. The effectual fervent prayer of the righteous man availeth much." I have a problem with pride and I would like to ask you all to pray for me. So stop where you are for just a moment and pray that I can fight and overcome pride when it rears its ugly head. I in turn am praying for all those who read this or hear my voice. You've got to understand that there is a difference between ignoring your problems and not having a desire to change your problems. If you don't have a desire to change then that's another story. If you do want to change, you should not ignore it; instead, you have to know the scripture and God's Word in addition to His Will. Just ask for help among the saints. People will pray for you if you ask, and you should ask.

After seeking help among the saints, you should help others. When God told me that my problem was pride, I said, "Well Lord, how do I handle it? What do I do about it?" When God tells you something, if you're earnestly seeking, He'll give you an answer. He said, "Service of the lowly." Where would I find "service of the lowly?" He said "Buttermilk Bottom."

For those of you who don't live in the Atlanta area, "Buttermilk Bottom" is an old catch phrase or slang referring to a place that represented the bottom or the deep ghetto. When I received that answer, which was years ago, I told my brother James about it, and we actually got in the car to go to "Buttermilk Bottom." I remember my father telling me that he used to throw newspapers there so I knew exactly where it was.

When we got there, we rolled down the window and asked someone if this was "Buttermilk Bottom." The man said, "No, no, no, it's on the other side of town," and so we drove to the other side. When we got there, we asked a few people if we were at "Buttermilk Bottom" and they said, "No." We went to at least four different places until I began to realize that "Buttermilk Bottom" is everywhere. I realized that there was probably a "Buttermilk Bottom" right down the street from my house or my job or even church. "Buttermilk Bottom" was just a nickname for people in need.

When you help the lowly, it will help you to reduce your pride. When you get down with people who really need help they can't pay you for it. Often, they won't really praise you for it, so your pride does not show itself. When you're helping people who have no means to spread the word to the mainstream and no one else knows, pride cannot show itself. Even more so, your pride will face people who are so far from God that they will criticize your good works. You won't get the same respect that you would if you were at home where people know who you are. So God was telling me to get around some people who really need you, who might not praise you or shower you with anything in return. As a matter of fact, when you leave they may feel you didn't do enough. I tell you, helping others at the "bottom" is what you need to do to control your pride.

I never went to work in "Buttermilk Bottom," but I know I still have to go. As a matter of fact, I was driving through downtown about a year later and I saw a sign right in front of the civic center and there a little green sign read, "Buttermilk Bottom." Most of the houses that were in the slum range have now been torn down and replaced with nice condos and town homes, but I understand the concept of what God was telling me when He said, "service of the lowly."

Do you remember what the disciples asked Jesus when he got down, took a basin of water and began to wash their feet? The disciples began asking, which among them was the greatest. They asked, "Lord which one of us can cast out these demons the best? Lord which one of us can deliver the Word the best? Which one of us can heal the best? Lord which one of us is the greatest?" They were asking out of a spirit of pride.

Pride affects everyone. Jesus says those among you who would be great must be the servant of all, and then Jesus got down and washed the disciples' feet. Now back in those days, they didn't have alligator shoes with socks, they had sandals and they walked in dirt, so Jesus was washing really dirty feet. Jesus got down and washed some dirty, mud incrusted feet that I'm certain did not have the best smell in the world. He did this to show the disciples how to deal with pride and how to move into a spirit of humility. How dirty are you willing to get to fight pride? It's something that all of us need to do.

As you read the daily proclamation, "O God I can do nothing successfully without you," remember the key word is "successfully." I'm sure all of us can do some things without God, but we can't do anything successfully without God. If God is not in it, it is destined to ultimately fail in one form or several forms. "I can do nothing successfully without you O God."

I leave you with this final verse in Romans 12:16. It sums up the spirit of humility. It simply says, "Live in harmony with each other. Don't try to act important, but always enjoy the company of ordinary people and don't think you know it all." (New Living Translation) That's the verse. We all have some work to do in the area of pride.

Reducing your pride will help you with all of the emotional hurt, which we know comes both fundamentally and psychologically from our ego. When you are humble you can't get hurt too easily. Pride will inevitably make you sensitive to everything. You become sensitive to every little criticism that comes your way, even when the criticism is helpful and constructive. All hurt fundamentally comes out of ego, emotional hurt. So if we can learn to put all things, our success and our failure in God's hand, it will reduce our pride and increase our humility. It will reduce your sensitivity and as a result your pain. The Bible says that pride precedes a fall; and if you're not real proud, you can't fall very far. Stiff necked saints, get limber in your neck and you can start by bowing your head in prayer.

It's Me!

Now you see that pride is universal. It's something that everyone struggles with at some point, even a Pastor. It is a real "thing" whose one goal is to consume us and stroke our ego to the point that we feel it was us the whole time and never God. We always need God. God is the reason that you and I even exist. He has ordered our steps. Remember to always give Him the praise for that which you have and for that which you have accomplished. If you feel pride coming on, don't give up...fight.

Proclamation for Pride

Number One: I pledge to read this statement aloud each morning and night and it will take root within my heart. This helps to reduce my pride and helps me to realize that I can do all things through Christ who strengthens me and that I can do nothing successfully without you O God.

Chapter Three

Envy: You Got It, I Want It!

By C. Elijah Bronner

"You got it, I want it." We normally don't say it, but we're thinking it. James 3:14-16 begins, "But if ye have bitter envying and strife in your hearts, glory not and lie not against the truth, this wisdom descended not from above but is earthly, sensual, devilish." Think about it, the word "devilish" means "demonic." Isn't that interesting? The Bible is literally describing the word "envy" as "demonic," earthly, carnal and fleshly, but ultimately its roots are demonic. Verse 16 says, "For where envy and strife are, there will be confusion and every evil work."

Romans 13:13 says that we should not get involved with envy. Galatians 5:26 also says that we should not get involved in envy. Proverbs 27:4 says that "Wrath is cruel, anger is outrageous, but who could stand before envy?" We may not have already been aware that envy ranks with wrath and anger, but now that we know it, we should work to resist it.

Proverbs 14:30 says that "A sound heart is the life of the flesh but envy is rottenness in the bones." The definition of envy is "the feeling of displeasure produced by witnessing or hearing the advantage or prosperity of others." Unfortunately, envy is a feeling of displeasure when you hear that somebody else has been blessed. The spirit of envy has roots in our Biblical history.

Cain killed Abel because of envy. Cain wasn't upset that

God didn't accept him; he was upset because God accepted Abel, and he couldn't bear the good fortune of Abel. Envy drove him to the point that he killed his own brother. He allowed envy to drive him to murder. There is no piece of good news which should produce a feeling of displeasure. Envy should not drive us to gossip. It should not drive us to speak failure into the lives of others, and it certainly shouldn't drive us to murder. We should not envy; we should rejoice.

Years ago at a family reunion, one of my cousins gave a testimony about having been blessed with a job with a six-figure income. Underneath the clapping and smiles was a very thick spirit of envy, evidenced by the later conversations which I overheard throughout the day. The envy was like a vapor rising up from the ground. As I sat there in the room there was no rejoicing, no celebration at the news. It was as if we had just been delivered some very awful, tragic news. Someone else's good fortune resulted in jealousy and envy gripping all of those around her. They were angry because someone else got blessed.

Well, that's what the spirit of envy is. It's that spirit on the inside that says, "That should be me, that should be me getting that, I'm supposed to get that, I'm next in line, that's what I wanted." Are you guilty of envy? How many times have you thought, "That should have been me, I should be making that, I should have gotten the promotion, I should have gotten the job, I should have gotten the new house, that's the car I wanted?" If you find yourself being angry at the success of someone else, particularly when you have not excelled in that area, you need to learn how to eradicate envy from your life. You should instead rejoice with them. Rejoice with those who rejoice!

I remember being in Sunday school many years ago when someone came into class and announced that one of the ladies at church was expecting a new baby. Everybody rejoiced... except for one lady. She ran out the room and burst into tears. When we went to find out what happened she said, "I want to get pregnant. I haven't been able to get pregnant. Everyone else is having a baby but me. That should be my baby." I was too young to understand the spirit of envy, but I now recognize it.

Envy is not the same as jealousy. They are very close, but they are not the same. Jealousy says I *want* the same as you have, but envy says I want to *deprive* you of what you have. Jealousy says I want a husband like yours; envy says I want your husband. Do you see the difference? Jealousy says I want a car like yours; envy says I want your car. Jealousy says I want a house like yours; envy says that should be my house. So envy looks at the blessing and the prosperity of others and it says *you got it, but I want it.* You have what I want. Envy really seeks to dispossess another and to take another's blessing.

Let me do you a favor: I will not pretend that I have never felt the spirit of envy. It may be difficult to believe that ministers struggle with sin and spirits, but we do. I am still human; I fall; I make mistakes. I know it's hard for some of you to believe that but it happens.

There was something that I had been really wanting for a long time and had actually been talking about it for years, but I wasn't in a position to get it at that time. So I just dreamed about it and talked about it and dreamed about it and talked about it. All of a sudden somebody whom I knew got what I wanted and when I got news of it, something hit the pit of my stomach, and it wasn't joy. I was angry because I'm the one who had been talking about it for years. I've dreamed of having that and then all of a sudden someone else popped up and received what I've always wanted. That thing should have been mine and it wasn't fair. I didn't know it at the time but the spirit of envy had crept in, and if you are not careful it will creep in on you and you won't even realize it.

The Bible says, in Romans 12:5 to rejoice with them who do rejoice. One translation says when other people are happy you get happy with them. Share in the happiness of others. That will keep you out of envy. Rejoice when others rejoice. Don't get mad just because someone else got something that you have always wanted. Rejoice because when you rejoice you're saying, "God, they got theirs now I'm next in line. We've gotten their blessing out of the way so now it will be sooner for me to get my blessing."

When you're rejoicing, you're sowing into the happiness and good fortune of somebody else, which someday will be rewarded and returned unto you. When you rejoice with them, when your day comes you'll have somebody to rejoice with you. Rejoice and get happy with other people. It's freeing to share in the happiness of others.

If you think about it, it was envy that caused Jesus to be

delivered over to be crucified. He was delivered to his executioners because of envy. The chief priest and the scribes were envious of him. The crowds of people were no longer talking about the priests and the scribes; they were now talking about Jesus. They were now saying, "Have you seen him? Have you heard the wisdom from Heaven? There's a Teacher among us. Have you seen the miracles? The lame are walking. The blind are seeing. The dead are being raised. Hear his teachings."

The kingdom of God was here and their jealousy of wanting to have power like Jesus turned into envy. The crowds left them and began following Jesus. These men weren't just jealous of his ministry, they were envious of his ministry. They said, "that should be us. They should be praising us. No one is coming to see us anymore. We haven't done any miracles. We don't have any signs. Everybody is following him." It was because of envy that they delivered him, prodded him and had him crucified. All of this took place because of the mentality, "you got it, but I want it." When you feel that way, envy is talking to you.

Envy involves three stages. It first involves discontentment, becoming dissatisfied with what you have. How do we become so discontent? It's because we're so busy looking at what everybody else has that we begin to compare. You see somebody who has something better than you and then you start not wanting what you have. You become dissatisfied with what you have because you spend so much time looking at somebody else and what they have. You start comparing. But let me give you this advice: you may not have everything you want but you should start wanting everything you have. When you start wanting everything you have, you begin to eliminate and combat envy. Be thankful. I don't have a Mercedes like Pastor Nathaniel but I've been happy just to ride in it. As nice as it would be to have what he has, I am very thankful for what I have. I have a sincere desire for those things that I already have. Having that desire and appreciation keeps envy from creeping into my life.

You have to stop comparing and start wanting what you have. Thank God for what you have. It may not be much, but I thank God I've got it. Thank God. Don't compare, don't compete, and don't complain.

After you find yourself in a state of discontentment, then you will begin falling into the second stage of envy - resentment. After you become dissatisfied with what you have, then you start having ill will toward the person who has what you want. You start resenting them because they were blessed and because they have what you want. So many relationships have fallen apart between friends and relatives because we have resented them for things that God gave to them.

The third stage of envy is covetousness. After discontentment and resentment, you will find yourself having a strong desire to possess another person's possession. You begin to covet what they have. Being dissatisfied with what you have leads to resentment of others who have what you want and that will lead to a strong and constant desire to possess another person's blessing.

When you start The 40 Day miracle, the proclamation to help us with envy says, "I will say nothing negative about anyone." Since I've been on The 40 Day Miracle, I've made a startling discovery. I found that I've been very quiet. When I had to eliminate gossiping and talking about people, I found that I didn't have very much to say. I didn't realize how much time I spend talking about other people. I spent a lot of days talking about church members.

Now that I have made a concerted effort not to gossip, I've found myself at lunch with my lunch buddy and we're just sitting there eating quietly with nothing to talk about. Normally we're naming names and we're just talking about people. We were constantly saying things like, "Have you heard, did you hear about, guess what so and so did, man you won't believe this." We were just talking about people at work and people at church. We we're talking about everybody and it made for wonderful conversation.

Time goes by so fast when you're gossiping; but since I haven't been able to talk about people and gossip, I've just been very quiet. I never realized how much of my conversation and speech were consumed with gossip. I was so quiet that my wife would forget that I had come home. The second part of the proclamation requires you to give a compliment to someone daily, whether you want to or not.

If you eliminate gossip and talking about people the Bible says in I Peter 3:10 that you'll see good days and you'll enjoy life. It literally says that your life will be lengthened and your life will be better. You will have a longer life just by withholding your tongue from evil. So refraining from all negative conversation will not only keep you out of envy but it will enhance your life. This is promised in the Word of God.

The second part of the proclamation is to compliment someone each day. Ephesians 4:29 reads, "Let no corrupt communication proceed out of your mouth. But that which is good to the use of edifying and that it may minister grace to the hearer." So in other words, you shouldn't say anything unless it will build, bless and benefit other people. This means your words should help and encourage people, and lift their spirits. A compliment will easily build, bless and benefit.

By giving a compliment you have the power to make an emotional deposit into somebody's bank account that will brighten their day and improve their life. Simultaneously, that same compliment is going to pay rich dividends into your own emotional bank account. You will find that when you compliment people not only do you make the person feel better, but also you are going to feel better yourself because you are concentrating on good things.

When you focus on positive things, you will find your own life becoming more positive. You will find yourself looking for the good in everyone you meet. You feel good when you bless someone and you walk away thinking about the way their eyes looked when you complimented them; the way they smiled; the way you made them feel. So even though you make an emotional deposit into their bank account you also receive dividends back into your own bank account so both of you walk away happy; both of you walk away full of joy.

I read a story about a woman who was very depressed and whose life was going down fast. She had gone through a terrible divorce and she had just been diagnosed with skin cancer. Her life was just quickly spiraling out of control and someone shared a simple concept with her which changed her life. She was instructed to take five pennies with her everyday when she left home. She was told to put them in her left pocket and during the day, she was to compliment somebody. After every compliment, she would take one penny for each compliment and then put it in the right pocket. She said the object was to have all five pennies in her right pocket before she returned home at the end of the day.

As silly as she thought it would be, she said she literally began to go on compliment hunts. She would seek people out to build, bless and benefit with her words. She would go to the grocery store and compliment the clerks, and she would go to restaurants and compliment the servers. She would give compliments at the gas stations, at work, at home and even to her long time friends. Wherever she went, she would be on the hunt for someone to compliment. Whether it was a smile, whether it was a hairdo, whether it was the way somebody was dressed, whether it was an attitude, whether it was a good deed that they were doing or a good job they were doing, she looked for something that she could say which would be a blessing.

She learned that if you look hard enough, you'd be able to find something about everyone to compliment. Sometimes, she found she didn't have to look hard at all.

Even the devil has a characteristic which we can compliment; he is very persistent at what he does. He persistently tries to destroy us if we let him. He persistently attacks us as the Bible says, to "kill, steal and destroy." He is persistent. If the devil can be complimented on one thing, then everybody you know, meet and come in contact with can receive at least one compliment from you.

Try it. Just make an effort to compliment people instead of tearing them down. Positive living and thinking cannot coexist with envy. If you begin seeing the positive things about other people and rejoicing at the blessings of other people, envy will have to pack up and move out. You are going to be free and enjoy life and the blessings which God intended for you to have.

Remember, want what you have and desire those things that God is giving to YOU and compliment, compliment, compliment. Mark Twain said a man could live for two months on one good compliment. If somebody looked at you and said "You're losing weight aren't you?" you could live for 3 months on that one compliment. Your words have power. Use them wisely, be positive and see how they will bless and empower your life.

I was in a store one day trying to buy some new pants. I had a very nice saleswoman who walked around with me to show me the various styles and to help me figure out which would be the best purchase for me. We finally found a pair of pants that we both thought were just what I was looking for. Were it not for the following magic words I would have just left them hanging in the store. She said, "Not everybody can wear this style of slacks, but looking at you, you have the physique and the muscular build to wear them."

I don't know if she was just making a sale or not, but her compliment went a long way. I almost bought every pair the store had and to this day, those are the only style of slacks that I buy. I bought them because of her one compliment. The power of a compliment will destroy the envy within you.

It's Me!

Wow! Instead of "you got it, I want it," we've just learned to say, "I got it, and I want it." Discontentment is the first stage. That means if you can enjoy and be grateful for those things that God intended for you to have, resentment and covetousness will not be a part of your life and envy is only born when all three are manifested within you. Just start loving what you have and make sure to find something positive in everyone you meet. It makes life a little less stressful and a whole lot more fulfilling. Compliment someone everyday.

Proclamation for Pride

Number Two: I pledge that I will compliment someone each day and will say nothing negative about anyone. Each day I will find and tell someone something good or great about themselves. I cannot count the compliments of the same person more than twice within any one week towards this pledge. I will not gossip or make negative statements of any kind about another person. This combats envy as it focuses me on others and gears me to be happy for them instead of focusing on myself.

Chapter Four

Gluttony:
The One Sin You Cannot Hide

By Nathaniel H. Bronner Jr.

By this time, you should have a pretty good handle on pride and envy. So far, we have dealt with two sins that people cannot readily tell that you possess. They can assume, but they cannot see them. This chapter deals with gluttony, the one sin that people will be able to see. Proverbs 23:2 says, "And put a knife to thy throat if thou be a man given to appetite." The NLT says, "If you're prone to overeating, put a knife to your throat." Now that seems kind of harsh, but that is literally what has happened in modern society.

If you go to the newsstand now virtually every magazine will have an article about losing weight and staying healthy. Just go check. Go to any magazine stand and look at any of the mainstream magazines that are not in a specific technical area and you will see something about weight loss. You don't even have to turn to the table of contents. Most of these magazines advertise on the front cover that there is a section in the magazine that can help you deal with weight loss. You probably won't see any weight loss articles in magazines that deal with boats and other things, but every other major mainstream

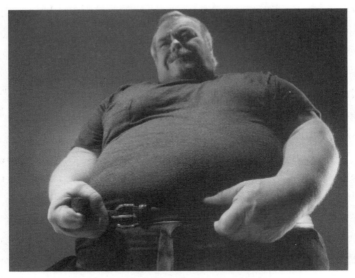

magazine will have something about weight loss.

I was looking at the August 2004 issue of Newsweek and it's entitled, "When Fat Attacks." The article deals with the scientific and technical explanation of the fat cell and why the fat cell is so difficult to deal with. As it goes through all of this scientific stuff it boils down to one simple fact, you have to eat less and exercise more. When you deal with any weight loss expert, I don't care what their specialty is, the underlying technique and explanation is all the same; you have to eat less and exercise more. I don't care how they put it, whether they call it low-carbs, high meat or low sugar; it doesn't matter. You have to eat less and exercise more. That's the whole weight loss industry in a nutshell and nothing else works.

One of the companies that I own is a health food company. We make a weight loss product called Cerum 7™ at Cerum7.com. It works, but it removes only an average of 8 pounds. Cerum 7™ is simply a product to get you started and get you motivated. Once you've lost the 8 pounds, the rest is up to you. The difference in our product and the other products is that we let you know up front that the product is NOT for permanent weight loss. Even to keep the 8 pounds off, you have to keep taking the product. Want permanent weight loss? Then you've got to eat less and exercise more. Proverbs says just that, "And put a knife to thy throat if thou be a man given to appetite." You have to be able to control your appetite.

In order for you to work anything properly, you should first have an understanding of it. You cannot control your appetite without understanding the digestive system. The digestive system begins with the mouth and it ends with the anus. It sounds gross, direct and probably even like I've given too much detail, but it's the truth. Your digestive tract is one long continuous tube. It's one long tube that starts in the mouth and travels through the throat, the esophagus, the stomach, the small and large intestine and the colon. It is all one long convoluted tube of about 30 to 35 feet long in the average American adult.

Doctors have taken their knowledge of the digestive system to develop a weight loss surgery called gastric bypass surgery. Gastric bypass surgery is when your stomach is cut open by a doctor and then they go in and suture or staple your stomach shut. If our stomach was as big as a basketball they staple it down to the size of a baseball. Remember, the digestive system is one long tube, which means that the throat and the stomach are one. So again, "and put a knife to thy throat if thou be a man given to appetite."

America is following that if you cannot control your appetite, the only other solution is to go in and cut you with a knife and cut your throat. So even though it was old Biblical scripture, that's exactly what we have done in the modern.

Now I don't recommend gastric bypass surgery because any major surgery has some major stuff that can go wrong, but if you can't control your appetite it's better for you to have gastric bypass surgery than to have all the excess weight that's even more detrimental to your health. This chapter on gluttony is kind of deep and rough, but it is necessary.

First of all the problem was best summed up by *Charisma* magazine. One of our pastors, my brother Pastor James, preached a sermon on the 8 keys to optimal health and he brought in an actual copy of the magazine. I really admonish everyone to go and read this. You can find the article online at charismamag.com. It's the July 2004 Issue and the entire issue is devoted to one thing and it has one thing on the cover.

It says, "Why is the Church So Fat?" They probably should have used more politically correct language like "Why is the Church So Overweight?" or "Why is the Church So Dimensionally Challenged?" Instead, they gave it to us plain and simple; "Why is the Church So Fat?"

Their estimates indicate that more than 400,000 people will die every year due to improper diet and inadequate exercise. They said if the current trends continue, by next year this number will grow and exceed 500,000 people, making obesity and being overweight the leading causes of preventable death beating out the once leading cause of cigarette smoking. When I did the statistics on a smaller scale, it came out to be that every day, 24 hours a day, over one person per minute would die from being overweight.

Medical experts say that every disease virtually known is made worse by being overweight due to the medical complications that obesity brings with it. The leading killers: heart disease, cancer, kidney failure and diabetes are all made worse by obesity. Even arthritis can get worse because you're overweight. It's too much weight on your frame. Everything is made worse by being overweight.

During a Sunday morning service, as I began to preach, I took a clear book bag and strapped it on in the front instead of putting it on my back. During the message and demonstration, I asked my brother to add bricks to the bag when I instructed him to do so. Leaving the congregation curious as to the meaning behind this clear bag, I continued delivering the message. I stated that at least 1 person will die due to excessive weight EVERY minute, EVERY day. At least 64.5% of Americans are overweight. That's virtually 2 out of every 3 people; 2 out of 3!

Charisma magazine says that although some groups are affected more than others, black women have more obesity than women of other races. Surveys show that blacks practice religion more than other groups. Studies show that obesity is highest in states with the highest religious affiliations. Southern Baptists have the highest weight and Jews and non-Christians have the lowest.

This is basically saying that the states with the most religious Christians are the fattest states. The race with the most religious people is the fattest race. The black women are fatter than the black men, but you'll notice, the women are far more religious than the men. So it's saying within the fattest race that is within the fattest religion in the fattest states, the gender that is the most religious is the fattest.

Basically the facts are saying that the more we practice traditional Christianity, the fatter we become. The statistics also show that the fatter we are, the sicker we are. So by that same correlation, the more we are Christian and the more we go to church, the sicker we are getting.

People can't you all see that there's something wrong with that picture. If you're honest about it, you really don't need books or statistics; you can just go to church and look around. Sorry, but it's true.

You cannot hide gluttony. It's the one sin that you cannot hide. I know this may be rough and may mess with your self-esteem at first, but hang in there. I would rather be rough and honest and change a few, than have you end up in the hospital because of something I didn't say.

The vast majority of cases due to obesity will cause all kinds of sickness. Your heart can't even hold up knowing it has to haul around a bunch of stuff. That's a major reason why heart disease and cancer are going through the roof, not to mention the increase in kidney failures. Being overweight causes the pancreas to flop and you've got to get on insulin. (The bricks being added are getting heavier and heavier to hold up)

But I'll say it again, I'd rather tell you this now and hope you listen than have you suffer and die early. There's no sense in not listening, ending up in the hospital and then calling on your pastor to come save you. Honestly, there's not too much a preacher can do if you have chosen to ignore this message. I'm sure your pastor will visit you, but he's probably not going to stay for very long.

Unfortunately and somehow, we have lost control especially in the church. Though sickness is not of God, the stats are showing that the more we go to church, the sicker we are getting. So something is wrong. We're missing the knowledge and we're missing the focus. It's causing us too much pain and it's causing us too much misery and a lot of this stuff is deeply rooted.

We're finding that those who are the healthiest and have the healthiest diet are able to control their appetite. They are slimmer and as a result they have less disease. It's sad that we, the body of Christ, are out of shape and overweight. How are we going to represent the body of Christ with bodies that don't look like Christ?

A revelation hit me this morning as I thought about it. In America, blacks are fatter than American Indians and American Indians are fatter than Hispanics and Hispanics are fatter than whites and whites are fatter than Asians. In the Asian culture, one of their dominant religions is Buddhism. Ironically, the statue of Buddha, the god they worship, is fat. They are slim and their god is fat.

Think about it. In every depiction that I have ever seen of Christ, He is always slender. So I began to wonder, how is it that the Asians who worship a fat Buddha are slender and Christians who worship a slender Jesus are fat? I said something's wrong. I have never seen a picture anywhere of Jesus with a potbelly; never. But every picture I see with Buddha, he's got this big old belly like a pregnant woman. What's wrong?

Charisma said that the first problem that we have in the church is recognizing that we have a problem. It sounds a little bit like chapter one. Pride won't let us admit certain things. However, no matter what the situation or problem is, it's very unlikely that we will address a problem without first honestly recognizing and admitting that we have a problem. When it comes to obesity in the church, we have failed to acknowledge it as a spiritual problem. We think obesity is a problem that the world has all of the answers to. We don't like to think of it as a spiritual problem. In other words, *Charisma* is basically saying, we're fat but we won't admit it.

When overweight people are around us, we feel comfortable. If 2 out of 3 people in America are overweight, then we need other overweight people around us to make us feel more comfortable. Soon, everyone is overweight and everyone is comfortable with it. As a result, according to the magazine, unsaved people who struggle with obesity may begin to believe that if God can't help Christians close the refrigerator, how powerful can He be? We need to lead them to Christ, but they are turned off by the thought of becoming overweight if they follow Christ. (My clear bag is still being filled with bricks, and it's definitely not getting any lighter.)

Why are we like this? It's simple; we conform to the land we are in. We found that out when we lost weight while vacationing in Italy. I lost weight when I went to Italy because everyone in Italy eats smaller portions than we do in America. We left dinner still hungry, but everyone lost weight. We didn't see any overweight Italians. Not that there aren't any, it's just that the average Italian was not overweight at all. They eat all of this rich food but they eat smaller portions. What they do is what The 40 Day Miracle instructs you to do.

In The 40 Day Miracle there is a daily proclamation that you must read morning and before bed. The proclamation that deals with gluttony says, "I pledge that I will stop eating before I am full. Health experts and medical research have long confirmed that we live longer and are healthier if we stop eating before we are full. Therefore I will leave the table still slightly hungry. This helps me to control the flesh's strongest physical craving which is food; it will certainly help me to control gluttony. Whenever I eliminate one thing, my body and mind has a tendency to compensate with something else. Often that compensation is food. I will stop eating at each meal before I am full." "Bring me another brick," I exclaimed.

We don't feel like we've had a good meal unless we can just sit back and pat our bellies. We like to eat to the point where we can hardly breathe. We love to pack ourselves. Medical research has proven over and over and over again that eating less will prolong the life of animals by 30-40%. This occurs simply by not letting the animals eat until they are fully satisfied.

Where did this behavior of eating until we are full come from in the first place? Much of it comes from parents who tell their children to eat until their plates are clean. We don't tell them to eat until they're full; we expect that whatever amount of food that we have placed on their plates should be gone.

God always places the natural instincts in you of what you should do if you can learn to listen to the body. That's why after children eat a certain amount they'll start doodling over their food and playing with it. They won't eat any more, but parents will say, "You'd better finish that food, better finish that food. Don't you know people are starving all around the world; finish that food." As a result we are trained not to leave anything on our plates, and even when we are full, we'll keep on eating, we'll keep on eating and we'll keep on eating.

Even in Pastor James' message, he showed where studies have proven that even when portions are increased, we still "clean the plate." If they bring small portions in a restaurant, that's all you'll eat. So often, instead of going to a restaurant and ordering off the menu, we will opt for the buffet or the "all you can eat" special. We feel like, "If I'm going to pay $10, I want as much as I can get. I don't want them putting a little bit on my plate." That's why in The 40 Day Miracle, in order to control gluttony, you must never eat until you are full. You must get up from that meal feeling slightly hungry. (Another brick has been added and they are really starting to pile up.) If we can learn to eat one serving and then stop, leaving hungry will help us lose weight.

Losing weight is not just an issue of health; it's also about emotion. Much of our weight is due to emotion. When we are depressed we eat; when we are lonely we eat; when we're stressed we eat. Food is a drug. It kills 30 times more people than all the illegal drugs in America put together including alcohol. Yet we'll look at the alcoholic and the drug addict and say that's just a shame.

Food kills 30 times more people than all of the alcohol and illegal drugs in America put together including the violence associated with it. It's so deadly that in the beginning, the first thing that God told Adam was what he should and should not eat. It was the first command given and it's still, even today, the deadliest thing that we do on a daily basis. (Go ahead and bring me another brick.) If we can learn to control our appetites, we'll learn to control so many other things in life. Let me tell you just a couple of things that you can do.

First of all you need to learn how to listen to your body. If you would for example buy some apples when you're hungry, and notice that there are only so many that you can eat. After you eat about 2 or 3 of them, the taste of the apples will change. Try it. This happens with virtually all food straight out of nature. As the body fills up and as the body gets to the point where it has had enough, by the body's standard not by the mind's standard, the very taste of the food will change. It does not happen with cooked food. With cooked food you can just keep on eating until you're about to burst. If you're eating fruit and uncooked food, the food will taste different.

When we went on the cleansing fast, I had some raw peanuts. I told my wife that these were some of the best peanuts

I had eaten in all my life. I even told her that they had to be the best peanuts in the world. I was just raving about the peanuts so much that she said let me try some. She got some and remarked that they were stale and didn't taste anything like I had described. Maybe they weren't as good as I thought, but I was just so hungry that they were the best in the world to me.

Hunger changes the way things taste to you. So by learning to eat more of the things God has placed in nature, without it being cooked, your taste for things will change. It will make such a difference that long before you even reach the point where the stomach is full, the mind will suddenly send you a signal saying you've had enough. When you get to that point people, you've got to learn to develop the discipline to say stop and not another bite.

The world tells us differently. Just look at the advertising. America has programmed us with catch phrases like, "Have it your way," "You can't eat just one," and even "Obey your thirst." You're NOT supposed to obey your thirst! Obeying our thirst is what gets us into most of the trouble that we get into. Obeying the body and the fleshly desires will always have you messed up. You've got to have an understanding of these things. You'll learn that for every meal during your 40 days, you will develop the discipline if you can just get to the point where you stop eating before you're full.

"Bring me one last brick," I instructed Pastor James. Now I know you're asking why I put all those bricks in the clear bag. I had nine bricks in this clear bag and it was heavy. Do you know what those nine bricks represent? The nine bricks represent the average American male and how much overweight he is. The average American man who is 5'9" tall is carrying around this much extra weight every day. Jesus said, "My yoke is easy and my burden is light." We aren't designed to carry all of this heavy stuff. While you're on The 40 Day Miracle, you will obtain the power to throw that stuff off. Taking the heavy book bag off felt a whole lot better. Taking off the heavy stuff in your own body will feel a whole lot better too. If I wouldn't carry this extra weight on the outside of my body, why would I want to carry extra weight on the inside of my body?

Maybe this is a touchy subject for you because you are overweight. Maybe it's a touchy subject for you because you find yourself changing from one diet plan to another trying to maintain a slender physique. I know it's difficult to deal with, but the fact of the matter is that if you fit into any one of these two categories, you are struggling with gluttony.

A lot of your problems with gluttony are because it is a spirit that affects your mind either with an emotional breakdown or from the brainwashing effects of society telling you to "Obey your thirst." I know gluttony is a spirit because I've experienced it; I know. Before I was married, and Pastor James can attest to this, God allowed me to experience the spirit of gluttony to the point that no matter what I ate or how much I ate, I just couldn't get full. Have you ever been at the point where you just couldn't get full? I could not get full and it stayed on me for weeks. I could eat two full meals and I still wasn't full. I told James I don't understand what this thing is. I just could not get full. Fortunately my body stayed slender, I never gained weight, but I couldn't get full.

God let me experience the actual spirit of gluttony. It's real. It's a spirit just like lust is a spirit. Now some of it is natural in the flesh but some of it is truly supernatural. We have to learn how to deal with it whether it is in the natural or whether it is in the supernatural. We have to get these spirits off of us. What happens to a lot of us, especially with women, is that we allow the spirit of gluttony to comfort us, instead of God. Gluttony has a magnificent way of filling the void of love. The difference is that since food can only temporarily fill the void, we have to go back for more, leading to obesity and triumph for gluttony.

God is trying to take us to a point where we can shed the weight and have a light burden. We've got to remember in our lowest emotional points that food cannot compete with God. God can do so much more for us when we're "going through."

We've also got to understand our own bodies. Some people can eat all day and not gain one ounce, while others can eat an ounce and gain a pound. Well not actually, but you get the point. Some of us can just look at food hard enough and feel the pounds adding up. Seriously, some bodies hold weight longer than others.

Having a body that's sensitive to weight is not necessarily a bad thing. My body has a lot more sensitivity than most people. To be honest, my skin is very sensitive, probably the most sensitive skin on the planet. People often compliment me on having beautiful skin. As a matter of fact, I walked in a restaurant not too long ago and the first thing the hostess said was, "Wow, your skin is beautiful; it's flawless."

I don't think my skin is flawless at all. Two days ago, I went to the health food store and purchased an 8oz. carton of Tofu ice cream, which doesn't have any dairy in it. Before I could finish that little 8 oz. carton of ice cream, I felt two bumps pop up on my face. My skin is so sensitive that it doesn't wait a week to react, bumps pop up on my skin while I'm swallowing.

Some people may see this as a bad thing, but I thank God for giving me an instant warning system when something's going wrong. These bumps help me to monitor my body and my life.

How many times has God given you a warning signal that you brushed off as a problem instead of a "red flag?" Whenever I'm eating something that I shouldn't be eating, God immediately let's me know it courtesy of bumps on my skin. God has placed within our flesh mechanisms that will warn us immediately that we're going over board. This warning is a blessing, but often, we don't see it that way. There are people in the world who have sensitive skin just like me, but they have acne everywhere because they choose to ignore the message that God is trying to send to us.

So now that we know gluttony is a big issue within the Christian church, we have to allow God to take the burden off of us. The 40 Day Miracle can help you break old habits like overeating. It will change you forever and you'll be able to push away. Stop eating before you're full even if you don't "clean your plate." We've been programmed that it's a sin to leave food on the table. It's not a sin. The sin is when we keep eating beyond what we're supposed to. It's better for it to go to waste than for it to go to your waist.

You've got to look at gluttony as not only a physical problem, but a spiritual one that manifests itself through your flesh. Often when we're dealing with issues that are spiritual, they require spiritual mechanisms to overcome them. I am in decent shape, but I still battle with gluttony. Gluttony is a very difficult sin to hide when it shows up in your gut, hips and thighs. I still battle with it because I still have a pretty big appetite right now. I still have a problem pushing away from the table, but The 40 Day Miracle has helped me tremendously and has kept me in good shape and good health.

The 40 Day Miracle will help you too by reminding you to stop eating before you get full. One small serving is enough.

Eating the rest of your food tomorrow isn't so bad. If you can just push away the minute you begin to feel that you've had what you know is enough and not just what you want, you'll develop the power to push away from the table and to conquer this thing once and for all.

According to The 40 Day Miracle, if you mess up and eat until you're full, you will have to skip two meals that you would normally eat. That's the sacrifice. Anytime you violate, you have to make a sacrifice that's going to hurt so that you don't make the same mistake the next time.

Who's going to know if you eat too much? You'll know. There's no need of you making a sacrifice that doesn't have any pain to it. If you really want to make a change, then be true to yourself. Remember the first step is always admitting that you do have a problem that needs to be changed and that can be changed. You can wear as much black and as many vertical stripes that you can find, and you will still not be able to hide. You can, however, get it under control. You can get your body under control. You can overcome the spirit of gluttony.

Paul said, "I have to crucify my flesh daily." What do you think he was talking about? He's saying he has to beat this thing "daily." Gluttony, like pride and envy, won't just go away; you have to battle with your flesh. If you have a problem overeating now, more than likely, the tendency to overeat will still be there 10 years down the road, but you can conquer it and it will no longer master you. The longer you stay away from where it masters you, the weaker its force gets over you.

God wants to break some things just in the spirit of gluttony. We're eating just too much and it goes along with being in the Promised Land. America is the land of plenty and when we have the land of plenty, we have a tendency to feast and feast and feast. One of the reasons why Asians are slender is because they don't have the kind of food we do.

All of us have weaknesses in the flesh. We all do. You have to first recognize it and then decide that today is the day that you will take back control. That's why the first line of that proclamation says, "Lord I surrender my will to Thy Will." Do you think God desires for you to be out of shape? Do you think He does? God wants us to represent His people. We are the body of Christ and if God wants it, we need to make sure that our will is lined up with His Will.

Food is no joke and it's literally "eating" away at the Christian church. It's not just the members; it's the Pastors, even me. While my brother, Pastor James was handing me the bricks, he said that something came over him. He said that he began to feel his body change and his stomach feel extra full. He said that he began to wonder what he had eaten for breakfast. With every brick he handed me, he felt his own stomach getting full as though he was about to pop.

Pastor James doesn't have a problem with gluttony; that's one spirit he's been able to keep off of him all of his life. As a matter of fact when he thought about what he had eaten for breakfast, he realized that he hadn't eaten anything since the previous night and then he'd only had 16 ounces of juice. He realized that it was the fullness of the anointing that God was placing on him and so I asked Pastor James to anoint those in the congregation who were truly struggling with gluttony. Although you are not in the sanctuary, I will share his prayer with you and ask God to move in your life:

The Fullness Anointing Prayer

Lord God our Father, You don't desire for your children to be sick. For even as earthly parents we know how it hurts our hearts to see our children sick, so Lord we pray this day for You to release the fullness anointing upon your people.

Lord as they stand here before You right now and as they listen over the Internet, CDs or cassettes or read these words, I pray O Lord that You send your anointing over them to rearrange even their stomachs O Father. For man sews up the stomach in the natural, how much more can You do in the spiritual than man could do in the natural for You created the belly.

And Lord we ask O Lord for supernatural gastric surgeries right now as I pray unto You. I pray that for those who hear or read these words, that You will touch them with your angels as I cannot be there to touch them. I pray those who are standing here that as I pass by to touch them that You will release the fullness anointing in their bodies that You'll perform a supernatural unseen surgery upon their stomachs to shrink the size, that they will be supernaturally full even before their physical stomach is full.

We believe in You O Lord; we trust in You. We have faith in You, O Lord that this thing is not too difficult for our God to do. In the name of Jesus we pray. Amen

I release the fullness anointing and I pray that you will feel full even before you get full.

It's Me!

I was hungry before I read this chapter, but not anymore. I understand that gluttony can be controlled, and it can be controlled by me. I think sometimes we forget that God gave us power over certain spirits and bad thoughts. It seems like an impossible task to pull away from the table, especially if there's still food on the plate. It can be done, and you and I are the people who can do it. We may be big physically, but we're even bigger spiritually and we can defeat this thing; we've just got to make it a daily thing.

Proclamation for Gluttony

Number Three: I pledge that I will stop eating BEFORE I am full. Health experts and medical research have long confirmed that we live longer and are healthier if we stop eating before we are full; therefore, I will leave the table still slightly hungry. This helps me to control the flesh's strongest physical craving which is food and helps me to control gluttony. If I have a tendency to overeat, I will listen or read once a week the message on gluttony and freely receive The Fullness Anointing at the end of the message. I WILL stop eating at each meal BEFORE I am full.

Chapter Five

Lust: Gotta Have It!

By Nathaniel H. Bronner Jr.

If you were sensitive to gluttony, you might want to move your feet because I'm probably going to be stepping on quite a few toes. It's a very real but sensitive and embarrassing sin that is not going to be easy to admit to. Most people don't admit to it until they've been found out, and even then they deny it to the end.

Lust, in the framework of the seven deadly sins is defined as an "inordinate craving for the pleasures of the body." Most of the time and in most of this modern society, when we think of the word lust; although it can apply to anything of the physical form, almost 95% of the time we're thinking about sexual things. Sexual lust can get you in a whole lot of trouble, especially if you're married. Lust is so bad in marriages these days that according to psychologist Bonnie E. Web, who has written several books on adultery, more than 50% of all married women at some point, cheat on their husbands.

Lust is not a new craze or a new "thing." Lust has always been a problem, even in the Bible days. As a matter of fact, years ago, when I was in college, a report suggested that 56% of all married women would cheat or had already cheated on their husbands. It was bad then, and it's still bad now. Just think, out of 2 married women whom you know, at least one of them has or will cheat on her husband during the marriage. You may be that one out of two. That's only what research says; one out of two. That's serious and proves how deep and powerful lust is. That figure is even true among married women in the church. We've got to know how to control it.

I'm sure we all know it's not just the women. What percent of married men do you think cheat on their wives according to the experts? According to the statistics, 70% of all married men will cheat on their wives. So out of 3 married men whom you know, at least 2 of them will cheat. That means that only one out of three is going to remain faithful to his wife. I know some of you still say infidelity only happens to couples who are not saved, but lust is everywhere, even in the church. Lust is not only as deep in the church as it is in the world; but according to the statistics, it's even deeper in the church.

According to a survey taken of Christian pastors in America, 12% of the pastors, that's 1 out of 8, admitted to having sexual intercourse with people other than their spouses whom they related to in their pastoral work. That means that 1 out of 8 of the pastors had sex with somebody in their congregations or on their staff. Hold on because it goes even deeper than that…I need to rephrase that…1 out of 8 pastors ADMITTED it. Lust is not just in the world, it's in the pulpit.

The survey went on to show that 18% admitted to sexual activity stopping short of intercourse with people in the church. Another 38% of the pastors said that they fantasized about having sex with someone other than their spouse at least monthly. A more recent article by Newsweek magazine noted that various surveys suggest that as many as 30% of male Protestant ministers have had sexual relationships with women other than their wives. Basically what the survey said is that if you are a pastor it cuts the percentage from 70% to 30%, still giving a horrifying statistic that 1 out of 3 pastors will not be faithful to their wives. So lust is right here among us.

My aunt who lives in a big city of another state recently told me that the community was in an uproar because the wife caught her husband, the pastor of a big church, in bed with somebody else. She was so upset with him that she went around telling everybody what happened and destroyed the entire Christian community in the city. The problem was not only that she caught her husband in bed with someone else; she caught her husband in bed with another male pastor. Lust is so real that if we don't get control soon it will tear up your marriage, the church, and ultimately your soul.

Romans 1:27 says "and likewise also the men leaving the natural use of the woman burned in their lust one towards another, men with men working that which is unseemingly." You see we've got some issues here. In I Corinthians 5:1 Paul is saying that the type of sex that is going on in the church is freakier than the sex that is going on in the world. That's what he said in a nutshell. So the church just as it was then still has a problem now. We have to learn how to get a hold of it and to control it. Lust is a serious problem among married couples and it's even worse among singles. It affects all ages.

I had to go see a man in the nursing home because he had gotten into some trouble. I found out that he had beaten up his wife. Why? He caught her naked in another man's room. This man was in a nursing home. He and his wife are well into their eighties. Eighty years old and they still have to fight lust proving that there is no age limit on lust. It happens at all ages, in all religious groups, in and out of the church.

One of the reasons why it is such a problem is that sexual desire is a normal state for a healthy person. It's normal. God implanted the drive in us for several reasons. First of all it is designed to give us the will to procreate. Out of all animals in nature, man is the only creature who has sex outside of the woman or female's estrus cycle. No other creature can have sex unless the female is in heat. But man? Man can have sex in heat, out of heat, cold, or hot, it doesn't matter. Man is the only creature who can have sex outside of the female ovulation or estrus cycle.

God placed the drive in us not only for procreation but also as a bonding agent. When you are sexually intimate with

someone, it bonds you to the person. So the sexual drive within us is a necessary, normal thing created by God. Sex was God's idea, but we took what was holy and what was pure and we have taken it to some new levels of perversion. We have entered into this thing a lot of lustful stuff that's just not supposed to be.

Actually the desire even in men for multiple partners is inherent in the flesh. That's why when you read about the kings in the Bible, almost every one of them had multiple wives. Many times when men hear about another man who has 10 wives he starts smiling and thinking about it. It is a natural part of the inherent part of the flesh. Men may smile, but women think differently. No woman desires five husbands. Well, she may want five different husbands, but never at the same time. So it's part of the male's natural composition; it's just in him. That's why infidelity ratios among men are higher than with women. However, I must admit, percentages for women are getting closer and closer to that of the men. So now that we know, what do we do?

Lust is one of the seven deadly sins during The 40 Day Miracle that you will not be able to eliminate. You will only be able to control it. Since you cannot eliminate the thought from your mind, there's nothing concrete that I can give you to eliminate it completely. If you're honest with yourself, some thoughts, no matter what you do, you just can't get rid of. You just can't fully stop. So you have to deal with some things concretely and other things in a practical way.

This is the affirmation that must be said twice a day dealing with lust, "If I am doing this, I pledge that I will stop having affairs, committing fornication, looking at pornography, or communicating with a person who is not my spouse or who is an ex or someone whom I flirt with. This helps to control the lust in me." This is what we will do during those 40 days but I am going to give you some additional keys and background on how to do this.

I know The 40 Day Miracle works because it worked for me long before it was devised. I had a problem with lust. As embarrassing as it is to admit it, it's the truth. I struggled with lust for a long time before I got married. When I was single, I was the typical male, running around with the typical problem of lust. Plain and simple, I had a difficulty handling sex. I was in the mindset of "I gotta have it."

I woke up one day and I realized that I needed to change my behavior. I wanted to change because I knew that I was causing heartbreak for other people who had invested their emotions into me. I said, "I can't do this to women. I've got to make a change." The second thing that I realized is that if I ever wanted to get married and stay faithful to that one woman, I needed to get control of lust right then.

If you don't get the demon of lust out of you now, it will stay with you in all of your relationships, even in your marriage. The preacher says, "I now pronounce you man and wife." He doesn't say, "and I cast out this demon of lust." If you have a demon of lust walking down the aisle all dressed in white, he will be at the alter when you get there, putting a ring on that finger when you say I do and signing the certificate right beside your name. The lust demon will stay with you as long as you do nothing.

Once I realized that not only was I hurting people and threatening to ruin my future relationship when I got married, something was placed in my spirit. It said, "You've got to go without sex for 40 days." I remember I told some of my good male friends that I was about to go without sex, without a woman, for 40 days. They just laughed at me and said, "You can't do it. You can't even be committed to one woman. How in the world are you going to go 40 days with no woman?" So while I was saying I could do it, they were saying I couldn't. But

I made a decision and I was sticking to it. That's what the second part of 3D Vision is in The 40 Day Miracle. You must decide. I made a decision. I said I am going to go with no woman for 40 days.

I decided. I called up all my girlfriends and said, "Look, I can't see you for 40 days." That's exactly what I did. I knew I had to separate. I told them not to call me, don't stop by; I was separating. I made up my mind, I set myself with determination, I started out and I made it two weeks and broke down. That's an important fact to know. You may mess up and break down during your 40 days, and some of you will. If you mess up, start over. That is so important. You must do a full 40 days. So if you mess up, start over. Think about this, if God granted you another 40 days, He's blessed you with another opportunity to finish. I can't say it enough, **if you mess up start over!** You must complete the full 40 days. There is power in the Biblical significance of going the 40 days.

So I messed up, but I had decided to go 40 days so I started over. Once again, I called the young ladies up and pleaded with them. I said, "Look, I'm going to do this so don't you call me." The second time I went about 4 weeks and messed up again, but by the third time… and people let me tell you when I went that 40 days, I can't scientifically explain it, but something snapped within me.

Something happened to me. I changed the grip that it had on me and it was almost like it broke. It couldn't handle me anymore and I was never the same. As a matter of fact, when I got to the 40 days I didn't even have an immediate desire to start back up with the women. I honestly told them to leave me alone because I was through. I can't explain it; when I got to my 40 days, something happened. It was like the grip of the demonic had broken and a grip of the flesh had been snapped. Even though I slipped after 45 days, it was different. I was in control. It never had a grip on me again. From that, I took one step at a time and changed. A year later, I was able to make a commitment to be celibate for 3 years before I got married. Those three years weren't easy, but they were easier than before since I was now in control. I was only able to do it after going through my 40 days.

That's why I tell you, you can do this and have a different life. Discover what it is, decide you're going to do it, and then do it. You will not be the same. Some of the old evil demonic stuff that's been gripping you, making you do things, making you feel a certain way and making you behave a certain way can be broken. You can break it and loose those bonds. It's okay if you have to go through the wilderness. When you come out, you will be a new creature.

There are seven keys to controlling lust. You first have to make a covenant with your eyes. Job 31:1 says, "I made a covenant with my eyes not to look lustfully at a girl." Look in the mirror, look deep into your eyes and tell them, "Eyes I've got to make an agreement with you." You have to agree with your eyes not to look upon things that you know already will tempt you. Sometimes, if we just don't look at stuff, our desire for it diminishes even if just a little bit.

If you know you're going to go through this program for 40 days, you don't need to open up a scrapbook and look at old pictures. You need to make a covenant with your eyes. Don't go to places where you know someone is going to be who's going to make your heart start beating in that special way. You need to make a covenant with your eyes to simply say that I am not going to look upon the things that are going to cause me temptation. Even Jesus said, "but I say unto you that whosoever looks on a woman to lust after her has committed adultery already in his heart."

The second way to control lust is to remember that if your eyes break the agreement you made, don't react. If your eyes wander, don't react. Sometimes, when we make covenants, we slip. So even if somebody is walking by and they catch your eye, don't react. That's what messes us up. Sometimes when a man sees a pretty woman or a woman sees a handsome man, we become real holy when we see them go by and shout, "Jesus," but don't react. If you see them let them pass because once you say it, it sends a vibration to your flesh and your flesh will say I got them now. Don't react.

Next, you should flee temptation. Avoid it at all cost. Joseph ran out naked when Potiphar's wife tried to seduce him. Sometimes you can be in situations and no matter who you are or how holy you are, sooner or later you will encounter someone who will tempt you. To flee is to run. Run far and fast from temptation. You may be in a situation and there will be someone talking and something will just go all through you. You know what I'm talking about. You can be happily married and so in love, but this other person will have a way of making you feel all funny inside. Something will just go all through you. When that happens, you get out of there in a hurry.

Let me warn you, whenever you're faced with great temptation and you stay in the midst of it, you'll never be able to prove how strong you are, you will only verify your breaking point. So when you are faced with temptation, go the other way. The Bible says in I Corinthians 6:18, "flee from sexual immorality." As animals, what's built within us is called "the flight" or "fight syndrome" and when we see someone who excites us, it causes all the adrenaline and hormones to build within us, and it gets us prepared. Other sins, we are told to resist; temptation we're told to flee from it.

Another great and fun way to get in control of lust is to have sex with your spouse if you are married. If you're not married, then stay away from sex; but if you are married, you should have plenty of sex. If you are married, the "plenty of sex" thing applies to having it with and ONLY with your own spouse. Paul says "it's good for a man not to marry but since there is so much immorality, each man should have his own wife and each woman her own husband. The husband should fulfill his marital duties to his wife and likewise the wife to the husband. Do not deprive each other except by mutual consent and for a time so that you may devote yourself to pray."

What Paul was saying is this, if you're not praying, there's no reason to withhold sex from your spouse. You should never hold sex hostage from your spouse unless you are fasting and praying or are doing so for medical reasons.

If you study Proverbs, you'll find that the vast majority of Proverbs talks about the adulterous woman. Solomon was obsessed with the adulterous woman. Why? Because he had 700 wives and there is no way in the world one man can satisfy 700 wives. Even though he was as wise as he could be, he didn't have sense enough to know that he could not give out enough sex to satisfy 700 wives. That's why when you read Proverbs he's talking about the adulterous woman so much. His wives were cheating on him because he couldn't handle them. It's pretty simple. It's like this, if you leave home hungry, food is going to be on your mind. Have sex before you leave home if that's what you're craving.

Another important thing to understand is that it's not

always just about sex. In the book "His Needs, Her Needs: Building An Affair Proof Marriage," Dr. Haley suggests that marriages fail because the spouse has a need for an extramarital affair. Often the failure of men and women to meet each other's need is due to a lack of knowledge rather than a selfish unwillingness to be considerate. He identified 5 needs that women have and 5 needs that men have in a relationship. That's another sermon. But you must understand that most extramarital affairs are really not about sex at all, it's about other stuff.

Sex within a marriage has often gotten bad because of other stuff. You've got to understand what went wrong before the sex. Was it a lack of communication? The root of why people cheat is usually not about sex. Even when singles are involved in sexual relationships, they're often not really in it for the sex; they're in it for a lot of other different reasons. They're trying to gain popularity; they're trying to be accepted; they're trying to get in with the in-crowd. Some have inferiority complexes so they'll go out and give themselves and get involved in all this stuff. Usually, when you get to the bottom of the situation, often there's a lack in the love they're receiving. So you've got to understand the root causes to even be able to deal with it.

You need to count the cost. There are so many venereal diseases that are out there, not to mention getting pregnant and being responsible for another life for the rest of your life. If you're married and you fool around and have an affair, it's going to affect a lot more people than just yourself. Even if you and your spouse try to work things out, the trust will never be the same. What effect will it have on your children and how they handle relationships in the future? Count the costs.

Even with singles, there is the feeling of heartbreak and

sometimes embarrassment. Ladies, if you keep your dress down and your panties up, it'll be real difficult for your heart to get broken. It may crack a little, but never completely broken. It won't happen. Every woman who's gotten her heart broken has taken her heart into the bedroom as a single or in an extramarital affair. So abstain if for no other reason than to protect your heart.

More importantly, probably the best way to control lust is to get closer to God. Sometimes, all the logic in the world won't stop real lust. You must have some spiritual under-girding with it. Logic will use reason and reason will tell you to use a condom. Logic can and will get around every wrong and bad decision. Being closer to God and having a deeper relationship with Him is the only thing that will truly sustain you. You must understand the spiritual principle behind this, and you must know when you get closer to God it will keep you and it will protect you.

I'll leave you with this. My wife called me while I was out of town and she had a serious tone in her voice. It wasn't her usual uplifting tone of voice...nope...I could tell I had done something wrong. She said she found a condom in my suitcase. Not knowing at first what she was talking about, I froze trying to figure out where in the world this came from.

She began laying out all the facts. She started by saying how we've been married for 10 years, and we don't use condoms; but there in fact was one in MY suitcase. She wanted to know where did it come from and why did I need one. She had a great question and all the facts.

But that's the thing about God, if you're in His Will, He will bring important details to your remembrance. Thank God I was close to Him. I quickly reminded her that the condom was in a bag along with other toiletries. It was the same bag of toiletries that we received when we went to Italy, after we were notified that our own bags with our toiletries would be delayed for two days. When they delayed our bags, they gave us a toiletry kit to use including the one condom. "Do you notice that all of the items in the toiletry bag are not from the U.S." I asked.

Now what if I didn't remember where the condom came from or worse, what if I had bought it? What explanation could I have given except, "Honey, I don't know where that came from." Would she have believed me?

Simple misunderstandings or events like this bring complications into the relationship that will not only cause a division but undoubtedly create a lack of trust. Lust is a real monster to deal with but so are the other 6 of the 7 deadly sins. That's why they are referred to as deadly. Each one of them is a real monster to handle and that's why we are going into detail about each and every one of them. Once you've been able to handle these for 40 days, you will be able to handle them for the rest of your days.

If you are married, take a moment to find your spouse and hug them. Hugging them won't get rid of your lustful thoughts, but it certainly is a start. Hugging is a way to get close to your spouse symbolizing the need for understanding each other more. Getting closer to them spiritually and physically will help you move away from lustful thinking and lustful actions. Just get close to your spouse. Just give them a good hug for one full minute. If you want to stop the lust and to stop the wondering, you two have to get into oneness. God wants you to be one flesh, one mind and one spirit. Amen.

Some of you haven't hugged each other in years and you'll be surprised at what just a hug will do. If your relationship is strong enough, nothing and no one will be able to come between you. When men date other women and women date other men, you'll always hear them say, my spouse doesn't understand me; and when you all start moving further and further apart, you're only making room for someone else to stand in the gap. If you want to stop lust, you need to be able to communicate.

Every relationship has problems; it's not how you work through those problems, it's that you work through them that will matter. Don't neglect to work it out. I don't know anyone who has not had some marital problems and sometimes we just have plenty of them and sometimes every other day. Sometimes things get rough and then they'll go smoothly for a while and then they're rough for a whole season. You have to make a decision and the main thing of preventing lust from entering into your relationship is that you've got to hang on to each other. If you're both hanging on, it's real hard for anything else or someone else to pull you apart.

It's God's plan to keep man and woman together in holy matrimony, but it's the devil's plan to wedge you apart. We so carelessly allow so many things in this world to wedge us apart, keep us separated and mad and angry. While we're mad and angry, as a result, someone else comes into the midst and they destroy what we have. But it never comes from the outside, it always comes from the inside and it comes because both of you have let go of each other. Lust, You <u>DON'T</u> Have to Have It!

It's Me!

Okay, I'll be honest...well, not that honest; but I will say, it's a relief to know that we don't have to feel bad about our desire for sex. God designed us that way. However, we must remember that He did not design us to have sex or sexual thoughts about everybody we come in contact with. A great man once told me that a man has got to know his limitations. He was basically saying that we should never put ourselves in a position to be tempted. Don't forget to avoid tempting situations, even if you have to rearrange your schedule. And don't forget that covenant with your eyes!

Proclamation for Lust

Number Four: If I am doing this, I pledge that I will stop flirting, having affairs, committing fornication, looking at pornography, or communicating with a person who is not my spouse or who is an ex. This helps to control the lust within me.

Chapter Six

Anger: When Your Last Nerve is About to Go

By James Bronner

"I pledge that I will not get angry, curse or complain. I will not raise my voice in anger. Nothing small nor great shall make me angry or react in anger." Easy or difficult? How easily do you get angry? How do you react when you're angry? This chapter is designed to help you "when your last nerve is about to go."

All throughout the Bible, no matter how spiritual the people were, at some point other people got them to the point of anger. No matter how much they prayed and no matter how many scriptures they quoted, at some point, they all got to the point where their last nerve was raw and about to go.

Let's look at the first family. Cain's envy lead to anger and his anger drove him to the point of murder. He killed his brother Abel because of envy as described in a previous chapter, but he also killed him as a result of anger. Anger didn't stop there; it even had an effect on Moses. Remember when Moses hit the rock when God only told him to talk to the rock? He led the Israelites all the way through the wilderness, but even after all he had done for them, his anger still kept him out of the Promised Land. He couldn't get into the Promised Land because the people got on his last nerves. What promise is your anger keeping you from?

In II Kings Ch. 2, Elisha, the great prophet received a double mantle from his mentor Elijah; all of his power, all the signs, wonders, miracles and prophecies throughout the Old Testament. As he was walking down a path one day, some kids called him "baldhead." From that simple act of name calling, as we all know kids do sometimes, he got angry and in his anger, he put a curse on those kids. The Bible says that two "she-bears" came out of the woods and tore those 42 children to bits.

Forty-two children were killed because they called Elisha a name. Elisha allowed something so simple to make him so angry. They got on his last nerves and he just couldn't take it any more. What small things can people say or do to drive you to your "last nerve?"

In the book of Acts, Chapter 15, Paul, the same man who wrote two-thirds of the entire New Testament, had an argument with his good running buddy, Barnabus. Barnabus was the guy he traveled with, whom he considered to be his close friend. This was someone with whom he discussed his deepest thoughts. The argument was about whether or not to take Mark with them on a trip. From that point on they split ways, and I never in scripture saw where they traveled together any more after that spat about brother Mark. A friendship ended over a simple disagreement.

What relationships have you severed because of an argument? Even the apostles got on each other's last nerve about Mark, and they were ministers of the Gospel. Ephesians 4:30 says, "and grieve not the Holy Spirit of God whereby ye are sealed unto the day of redemption let all bitterness and wrath and anger and clamor and evil speaking be put away from you with all malice and be ye kind one to another tender-hearted forgiving one another even as God for Christ sake has forgiven you. Be ye therefore followers of God as dear children and walk in love as Christ also hath loved us and hath given Himself for us an offering and a sacrifice to God for a sweet smelling savor."

Jesus' whole message was about loving your enemy. When someone strikes you on one cheek He said present to them the other side. He said to love your enemies by blessing those who curse you, by doing good to those who hate you and by praying for those who despitefully use you and persecute you.

What do you think would have happened if Jesus had gotten angry while he was on the cross and reacted in the same manner as Moses or Elisha or even Paul? What curse would have been put upon all of the men who were spitting in his face? What blessings would the men who put these nails in his hands have missed out on? What relationships would he have severed with those who were putting the nails in his feet and lashes on his back? What do you think would have happened to the Gospel as we know it and to the history of our religion and faith if Jesus had gotten angry and acted out His anger? He had power to call down fire and brimstone from Heaven unto those people? What if He had gotten angry on the Cross?

When you really think about it, you'll admit, you never really forgive people whom you're truly angry with. It's very difficult to hold a grudge with hate in your heart and truly forgive somebody. But remember, the Bible says that if you don't forgive your brother, then God can't forgive you. We all desperately need God's forgiveness. We can't afford not to forgive others.

God doesn't even want your money if you're angry. He said to just don't even bring it. He would rather for you to leave it at the alter and get it right with your brother first. Now you know there's something wrong when the church doesn't even want your money. That's something serious there. The church might not put up with some things, but even when they're upset with you, they usually still want your money. But what happens if they no longer want to accept your money until you have gotten right with your brother first?

The scariest thing about anger is that we live in a society today where people get furious over just the smallest little thing. Sometimes when I stop at a red light and the person in front of me doesn't notice that the light is green because they are too busy reading or talking on the phone, I figure it's my responsibility to tell them to go. But before I get a chance to blow my horn, my wife will quickly remind me that even if I'm not blowing my horn out of anger, people may perceive it that way and shoot me for it so I've learned how to sit and wait. Okay, I haven't learned it completely, I usually only sit and wait when she's in the car because I understand her fears. Don't let it happen while I'm in the car by myself and the person won't go because they're not paying attention to the light. We should all want to avoid confrontation because we don't know how close other people are to their "last nerves."

At one of our company meetings, we sat around the boardroom table trying to come up with creative code words so that the person sitting at the front desk would be able to use code words over the PA system. We could communicate problems over the PA system without enraging an angry customer at the front desk who was already close enough to their breaking point. We knew an angry person might lose their mind if we said, "We've got a real crazy one at the front desk, send the big guys for back up." So we came up with two code words. The first one means, "I've got someone who's just a little irate and they can be handled calmly." The other code word means, "I've got someone who's about to break me in half so could you please send strong men to help me out. Now!"

We actually are working on a third code word that means someone has gone "postal" and they have come in "strapped." When we say "strapped," we mean they have a weapon and intend on using it. The best code word I came up with is, "RUN!" Basically, "run" means just that. It means, there's no need to come help me at the front because I'm gone and you should hit the door running fast as you can. Don't even come check it out to see what it is, just hit the door running. Leave your belongings on the desk; don't worry about the computer just run for the woods. As funny or as sad as it sounds, that was one of the major issues on our agenda because we understood that it doesn't take much to upset people these days.

We get angry so easily. When people at the United States Post Office lose their jobs, everybody gets scared. There was a point in time where every time a Post Office worker lost their job, they would come back and shoot everybody. It got so bad until people now say you're "postal" instead of you're "crazy." Even kids are shooting people for stepping on their shoes. Someone was telling me recently that while they were riding on the public bus system a young guy was almost stabbed to death by an older gentleman only because the young man asked to sit down beside the older guy. The older guy pulled a knife, just because of a seat.

People don't just get mad at strangers, but even parents are getting so angry with their own children that they are inflicting bodily harm to them. People are getting so mad with their own children that they are beating them to the point where they have to go to the hospital; all of this out of anger.

People are getting mad at their spouses and battering them and the women now are even battering husbands at the same rate that husbands are battering the women. Everybody's mad. Everybody's got a short fuse. People go to work mad at their bosses and then leave work mad at co-workers; just mad, mad, mad everywhere.

What makes us so angry? Simple things. If someone cuts in front of us in traffic, takes too long at the cash register, or gets our orders wrong at the drive thru window, we get mad and not just mad; we get angry. If somebody's driving the speed limit posted by law and we're late, we get mad at them for obeying the law. We don't care that it's not their fault, we just want to be mad and blame somebody for our anger. Even at church, knowing there aren't any assigned seats with the exception of the pastors, if somebody at church sits in the seat that we normally sit in, even if it's a visitor who doesn't know, we get mad. We don't hear anything the preacher says because we're not in our right seat.

Even the words we use to describe our anger have the results and the revelation built-in. If you analyze it and listen carefully, the things that we say casually have the end result of our anger built-in. Webster's dictionary defines mad as being "disordered in mind; insane." Insane is just the clinical word for just plain crazy. It goes on to define it as: completely unrestrained by reason and judgment, incapable of being explained or accounted for; carried away by intense anger, furious; carried away by enthusiasm or desire; infected with rabies. I use Webster's definition because sometimes the world has a deeper revelation of stuff than even the church. In other words, Webster is saying that in anger you're acting like a crazy man and like a dog with rabies.

God even showed me the revelation while I was in the bathroom. He showed me that even in the word " MAD," when spelled backwards forms the most common curse word that people say when they get mad. A curse word and not just any curse word, the very one that people say when they get mad, is built into the word "mad" itself. Sometimes we say that we are "mad as hell" or "you are getting on my last nerve," "you make me sick," "you're driving me crazy" or even, "you're gonna make me lose my mind." I've even heard Christians who are saved and sanctified get to the point that they will say, "you 'bout to make me lay my religion down" and they start pulling up their sleeves. What have we allowed anger to do to us, even as Christians?

Anger is contagious. When you approach someone and you are already angry or mad, your attitude of anger will only make him or her react to you with anger. It's a natural defense to give a rebuttal with anger when someone comes at you angry.

I went to a seminar recently that was hosted by Dick Gregory. During his lecture, he asked a woman of a different race, "What if I hated you solely because you are of a different race?" He went on to say, "Imagine if I had come to this seminar today planning to get you and imagine that I had been carrying around feces in my pocket for 3 days with a plan to come in and throw it on you? Imagine now that I'm carrying feces in my pocket and I get here and the sight of you has aroused my anger even further so I take it out of my pocket and throw it in on you?"

As graphic as he sounded, he asked her how long she would allow the feces to stay on her. She said that she would immediately go into the bathroom and wash it off. He said, "so in a few minutes you'd be rid of the same feces that I had been carrying around for 3 days? You mean within minutes, you would be rid of the very thing that I have smelled for 3 long days. Prior to throwing it on you, I've carried that feces in my pocket, smelling it everywhere I went; smelling it at work, at home with my family at the dinner table, in my bed and even when I got in my car to come here today. As a matter of fact my whole family had to smell it for those three days and you've gotten rid of it within minutes."

His point was to show us what anger is really like and how we carry it inside of us at all times; to work, to bed, to dinner, and even around our family. Walking around with anger and madness aimed at another person for one reason or another, thinking that we are doing something to hurt them by not speaking or by giving them a mean look is really only affecting us, causing us to "smell the feces" inside of us. Our household suffers when we're mad even if we're mad at someone else. Look at all of the innocent people who we end up hurting all because we are carrying the "feces" of anger around with us. It even pollutes our own bodies and causes illness.

An article from the *Better Health Channel* says that "anger triggers the body's fight or flight response. The adrenal glands flood the blood with stress hormones such as adrenaline and cortisone. As a result, the brain shunts blood away from the gut and towards the muscles in preparation for physical exertion causing the heart rate, blood pressure and respiration to increase. The body temperature rises and the skin perspires.

The constant flood of stress chemicals and associated metabolic changes that accompany recurrent unmanaged anger can eventually cause harm to many different systems of the body."

Some of the short and long term health problems that have been linked to unmanaged anger include headaches, digestive problems such as abdominal pain and ulcers, insomnia, increased anxiety, depression, high blood pressure, skin problems such as eczema, heart attack, stroke, and nervous breakdown. The kicker, what I have never heard or read before, but what was proven in several studies was that the hormone, cortisone, that is released in the body by anger causes an increase in appetite and increased fat accumulation around the stomach area.

It sounded a little ridiculous to me so I had to go and research it. There it was on *Web MD* and other health sites and medical journals. They said that the fat is not even general fat but that it somehow targets the fat around the abdominal area, which is the most dangerous area according to doctors for fat to accumulate. So maybe the next time somebody gets on your nerves, you need to just stop and say to yourself that I am not going to get mad because you are going to make my gut grow.

You need to think about that and say, "I've got to maintain my gut; I don't have enough calories to spare on you today." You need to think about these things the next time somebody gets on your nerves. Their findings also showed that the occurrence of high blood pressure had increased to an all-time high rate in the U.S. One out of three U.S. adults has high blood pressure.

Anger is one of the few sins that will secretly manifest a physical change. You can tell when some people get mad because their veins start popping out in their necks or under their eyes or the temples. That's when you really know that they are steaming when you can actually see it on them. Over time anger will even turn your hair gray and put wrinkles on your face. If you frown up long enough, those wrinkles from frowning will form on your face.

I've seen some people who look like they are just mad about everything but that's just how their faces are made just from being mad so many years. You ask them what's wrong and they wonder why you asked. They may even ask, "Should I be upset about something?" These people are as happy as can be, but they've put so much anger on their faces that the wrinkles from it have just stayed. I guess their wrinkles have decided, "Why keep going away, you're just going to get mad again, so I'll stay."

I'm going to outline 10 keys to anger management. If you study and retain these keys, you can spend more of your life being happy.

Take 10

In the midst of your anger, stop and take 10 deep breaths concentrating on the breaths themselves. If you think about it, anger causes your breathing to speed up. That's why we call it, "huffing and puffing" mad. On the flip side when you are sleeping or relaxing, slower breathing is induced. If you mimic how your breath is when you are relaxed, your body will automatically fall in line and begin to relax.

Walk

If you do get into a heated conversation, which we all will, take a walk outside. There's something about nature that's just soothing to the mind and spirit. No matter what it is; the trees, the lake or just the grass, just get out and get some exercise out in nature. It does a second thing by giving you some exercise. Exercise relieves tension and helps relax the body.

Pray

Pray for the person whom you are in the conflict with. I'm not talking about getting down on your knees and asking God to strike them down as Elisha did. I know you may want to, but don't. Some of us love to pray, "Lord you fight my battles and just cripple their hands with arthritis and give them some chest pains." I'm not talking about that kind of prayer, but instead you should pray a prayer of forgiveness and pray that God will help them with their personality. Pray for the person. It's hard to be mad when you sincerely and lovingly pray for them.

Cool Down

It's okay to cool down first and wait another day. Discuss the matter on a day when you've had time to think about it and cool down. It's hard to say the right things in the midst of your anger. When you get so upset, words just come out wrong, and we find ourselves trying so hard to take back hurtful things that we didn't really mean. Even if you don't mean any harm when you are mad, they can just hear it in your voice. It just comes out wrong. You never want to be in the position of saying, "I wish I hadn't said that." Your tongue is already the most dangerous part of your body. Why would you use it when you're angry? Marriages break up because the wrong thing was said.

Leave it at Work

Don't bring work anger home; leave it at the office. The first thing some people do when they come home angry from work is say, "You know this happened to me today and can you believe this person," and by the time they have reenacted the whole argument, they get heated up all over again and sometimes the spouse gets angry at the person at work and then everybody's on edge. If the spouse doesn't agree with your side, they must decide to stay quiet or voice their opinion and either of the two decisions will certainly cause a new argument between the spouses. So the anger is displaced; leave that anger at work.

Rest

When your body and nerves are tired, you're easier to get upset. My daddy said that the only thing right that you can do when you are tired is to rest.

Meditate

Learn to meditate on God's peace. This should not happen after the argument at the end of the day. You should actually start your day with meditation. This is a proactive approach to anger and not a reactive one. Most days when we get out the bed, we get out running instead of starting the day with prayer and meditation. It soothes the spirit. If you know there's a chance of rain, you take an umbrella just in case. There's always a chance of confrontation even if you never leave home, so you should have an umbrella of meditation just in case anger comes raining down on you.

Avoid, Avoid, Avoid

You learned that when dealing with lust you should not enter into situations that will tempt you. It's the same thing with anger; don't hang around people who you know are hot-tempered and easily angered. Proverbs 22 says, "Do not make friends with a hot-tempered man."

Forgive Before Bed

The Bible says that we should never let the sun go down on our wrath. My father said that in marriage always forgive the person before you go to bed. You can discuss it the next day if you haven't cooled down to the point of having the right words, but never go to sleep still mad at the person. Forgive them so that when you wake, you will have a new outlook on the situation. Never sleep on that anger.

Don't get Angry

Make a conscious decision not to get angry. Control yourself. My father was a very high-strung individual and I found myself with that same kind of lion on the inside of me. My father was truly one of a kind when it came to anger. I loved my father, but just being around him would make you tired. He was never able to keep a secretary for very long. I found that a lot of times the lion would stir up on the inside of me just like it would do in my daddy and I had to begin to monitor myself and catch myself whenever I found my voice rising or my temperature rising. I had to learn to temper myself and calm down and over time this began to change my very nature. So monitor yourself and control yourself.

If you practice these 10 steps and really work at it, you should be able to soothe the savage beast within you and change your life and the lives of those around you. Sometimes we get angry because we think we're right and we want the world to change to fit us; but a lot of times, it's us who need to be changed. If you'll change on the inside you'll find that things around you and people around you will begin to change.

It's Me!

I know you won't believe this, but as I was reading about anger, my husband came downstairs and started fussing at me because I was on the computer and he needed to get on the Internet. Normally, I would react, but I didn't. I apologized, stopped reading and went upstairs. He stormed out of the house. Normally I would say, "What's wrong with you? I can't believe you're acting silly just because I'm on the computer." But I didn't, I kept quiet, took a few deep breaths and thought about how much worse I would make it if I responded. My husband just called me a few minutes ago and said, "I wanted to apologize for getting mad. You didn't do anything. I guess I was just tired and took it out on you." Wow! It really worked! Controlling your anger causes those around you to get there's under control too.

Proclamation for Anger

Number Five: I pledge that I will not get angry, curse or complain. I will not raise my voice in anger. Nothing great or small will make me angry or react in anger. I will not complain about ANYTHING. Not the weather, not the government, not the news, not my aches, not my money, not my kids, my spouse, my job, my car, traffic, or anything else. I will NOT complain about ANYTHING!

Chapter Seven

Greed: A Swimming Pool in the Bathroom

By James Bronner

You're almost at the end of the book. This chapter deals with sin number six of the seven, which is greed. Today I am wearing three watches. Watches, while fashionable, were really only designed with one purpose in mind, to tell time. Some watches are digital and others are analog, but they serve the same purpose.

Why do I have three if they all serve the same purpose? Greed. It only takes one watch to know what time it is; instead of one watch, I have three watches on. Even though I am wearing three times more watches than the average person, I am gaining nothing more than what you would gain if you were wearing only one; no additional purpose is served. Many of us buy a second watch because our sports watch isn't appropriate when we're dressed up. Satisfied? Nope. We buy the third watch as our work watch because the sports watch is too casual and the other watch is too dressy. Satisfied? Nope. We say, "one more will be enough," but once we get that "one more," we say, "okay, just one more."

Being fulfilled with the things you have is very difficult

because of greed. The more we buy, the more possessions we have. I tried to get some watches on my ankle, but they just wouldn't fit. I tell you there is no limit to the material world and how far we'll take it.

In Luke 12:13, in the NIV version, it reads, "Someone in the crowd said teacher, tell my brother to divide the inheritance with me. Jesus asked, 'Man who appointed me a judge or an arbiter between you?'" Then he said to them, "Watch out, be on your guard against all kinds of greed. A man's life does not consist in the abundance of his possessions."

He then told them the parable of the rich man whose land produced good crop. The man wondered what he would do with all of his good crops since he did not have a place to store it. The rich man decided to tear down the existing barns to build bigger ones. He figured bigger barns would certainly hold all his grain and goods so that one day he can say that he had plenty of good things stored up during his years. He thought he would just take life easy, eat, drink and be merry; but God said to him, "You fool, this very night your life will be demanded from you. Then who will get what you have prepared for yourself?" This is how it would be with anyone who stores up things for himself but is not rich towards God.

The rich today don't build bigger barns, but they do build bigger homes to store their riches. I searched the Internet to find a large house that would be comparable to the wealth of the bigger barns as described in the parable, and I ask you, "do you have a swimming pool in your bathroom?" I'm not asking whether or not you allow your children to get in the bathtub in their bathing suits; I'm asking if you have a real swimming pool in your bathroom somewhere near the sink, bathtub, shower, closet, commode or Jacuzzi? Do you know of anybody? Well, just so you know, there are people in the world who have pools in their bathrooms. Even though this sounds excessive, we all have our own versions of "a pool in the bathroom" in some part of our lives that we can sum up as greed.

In Acts 5:1, the Bible says, "but a certain man named Ananias with Sapphira, his wife, sold their possessions and kept back part of the price, his wife also being privy to it and brought a certain part and laid it at the apostle's feet; but Peter said, 'Ananias why has satan filled thine heart to lie to the Holy Ghost and to keep back part of the price of the land? While it remains was it not thine own and after it was sold was it not in thine own power? Why have thou conceived this thing in thine heart? Thou have not lied unto men but unto God; and Ananias hearing these words fell down and gave up the ghost."

The phrase "gave up the ghost" means that Ananias died and as a result, great fear came on all them who heard these things. The young men rose, wound him up and carried him out and buried him. Peter asked his wife, Sapphira the same question, "Did you pay this amount for the land?" She agreed with her husband and she dropped dead too.

After searching the scriptures, I was given a revelation. These two stories that I just told you about are the only two places in the New Testament where God passed judgment immediately by killing them. Passing an immediate sentence on sinful acts was common in the Old Testament, but it happened only twice in the New Testament. Ironically, both cases dealt directly with mammon, material possession and greed. Even Jesus was betrayed by his own disciple Judas over 30 pieces of silver. Do you have a swimming pool in your bathroom?

I know you're thinking, I don't have a swimming pool in my bathroom much less one in my backyard. You may be saying well, greed doesn't apply to me because I don't possess a lot of things or money, but Timothy tells us those things that we should be satisfied with. In I Timothy 6:6, Timothy tells us "Godliness with contentment is a great gain for we brought nothing into this world and it is certain we can carry nothing out. But having food and clothing let us be therewith content. But they that will be rich fall into temptations and a snare and in the many foolish and hurtful lust which drown men in destruction and perdition for the love of money is the root of all evil which while some coveted after they have erred from the faith and pierced themselves through with many sorrows."

Timothy is talking about the dangers of the love of money and describing how both the love of money and greed go hand in hand as the root of all evil. Greed, like the other sins should be taken very seriously. But you must consider that greed was the only sin that God struck with immediate reaction in the New Testament. His reaction was not subtle; the punishment was immediate death.

Greed is the only thing that He describes as the root of all evil, and our society is not helping the situation. Our society is plagued with big corporations that seem to keep finding themselves in a lot of trouble with the government because of greed; reporting erroneous figures on the books. Drugs could be stopped in this country if it were not for the greed factor.

Greed is even affecting the churches and the preachers. Today, preachers get more excited about the amount of money in the offering than the number of souls being saved. The purpose of the church is not to raise money; it's to spread the Word of God. Ministers are now measuring the success of a revival in dollars rather than in souls. Many ministers today argue that the church is a business and cannot exist unless we focus on the church's ability to bring in a steady income. The goal of any business is to make a monetary profit; but the goal of ministry was never designed as a goal to make monetary profit.

Your life, your existence was not designed to be a business or a monetary profit making machine. What is your goal? You must know when enough is enough and how much is enough. Do you? Think about that for a moment.

How much will be enough for you?
When will you be satisfied?

If you went and bought the car of your dreams, would you be satisfied or would you still desire a new one in a few years? What is enough? What about your home? It was enough when you moved in; do you want something bigger? I can tell you right now that no matter what figures and things you come up with, after a few months if not weeks, you will desire more.

Rockefeller, the billionaire, when asked how much would be enough, he was honest and said, "Just one more dollar than what I have now." It didn't matter if he had 10 billion, 20 billion or 30 billion dollars. Enough would be 30 billion and one dollar. It illustrated so clearly the spirit of greed. Greed tells you that there's never a point when enough is enough.

We commonly describe sin as what is done in the closet, but what's actually in your closet can also show you what's in your heart. When you moved into your home, you probably looked around and even checked out the closet thinking, "I finally have enough space for my clothes." Instead of looking in your closet now and realizing that your closet is so full that the clothes are touching, you probably spend your time saying, "I don't have anything to wear!" Look in your closet again, if your clothes are touching each other, you should be able to say, "Wow, God has really blessed me." Your first reaction will give you some idea about your level of greed.

Greed is a root of a lot of other sins even though most of the time it's related to money. Gluttony is really the greed of food. Alcoholism is the greed of alcohol. Envy and jealousy look at what someone else has and get greedy. Sloth is a greed for sleep and relaxation. Promiscuity is a greed for sex. Pride is the greed of ego. Impatience is the greed for speed. And men, I'm here to tell you that the greed for women will get you in trouble too. If you don't believe me ask Brother Solomon in the Bible.

When I was in elementary school, the kids who were greedy at lunchtime would come around to the other kids' lunch tables and they would see something on someone's plate that they wanted. Even though these greedy kids had already eaten the exact same lunch, they would stick their hands or fingers in other people's food and ask, "Are you going to eat that; do you want that?" Some of the kids would be so disgusted that they would concede and say, "It's nasty now, just go on and take it; I don't want it anymore." Then there was always that other group who had a plan. When those greedy kids came to them and touched their food, they would pick it up, lick it and then say, "No, you can have it." So you see even in elementary school greed was forming in kids.

How do we combat greed? When I spoke about anger, I gave you ten keys; well for greed I am only giving you one.

That one key is giving. The opposite of greed is generosity. If you want to eliminate something, just begin to do the opposite a little more and you will find that your spirit will begin to change. Whatever you want to change, doing the opposite will make a difference. The spirit of greed cannot coexist with generosity.

The part of the daily proclamation in The 40 Day Miracle that deals with greed reads:

I pledge that I will give someone something material each day. The size does not matter. Whether it is a dollar or a donut or buying someone's lunch, I must give someone "other than my own children" something each day. At least every other day it must be someone OUTSIDE of my family. If I am a member of a church, during this period I will give to my church as directed by my church. Concentrating on giving helps me to control greed and realize my own blessings.

You will learn in the next chapter about making excuses, but with this proclamation, even if you are not a member of a church, do not allow that to stop you. You can give at VirtualChurch.com and help support the online ministry there if you don't have a church home. On The 40 Day Miracle, with the commandment to give and help others materially on a daily basis, your mindset will automatically shift. You will have a genuine desire to help.

When you're required to help somebody outside of your

family everyday, you actually become glad when somebody asks you for some help. Normally with a lot of us, if we walk down the street and see somebody on one side of the street who may look like they are in need, we will switch sides of the street without even one thought. Our mindset is, "If I pass by, he or she may begin begging me for something and I am not trying to be bothered." Some of us avoid these people at all costs.

The 40 Day Miracle tells you to avoid a lot of things, but helping others is not one of them. When you're on The 40 Day Miracle, after a few days, you will find yourself gravitating and actually going over to people to check on them and to see if there's anything you can do for them. There's a shift in your spirit.

The other day I was in the grocery store parking lot with my wife. When I chose to park further out from the store, my wife immediately let me know that there were parking spaces that were closer. She didn't know what I was doing at the time; I wanted to walk the distance because I saw a man who looked like he needed some help. Because I was on The 40 Day Miracle, it had changed my spirit and I was out to see whom I could help. I took the long way just so I could walk past this man, and I looked him in the eyes and asked him how was he doing and began to speak to him.

When he asked me for change, he addressed me as "minister." I wasn't wearing a pin or shirt that read "minister." Not only was he not a member of our church, but I had never seen him before. I could tell by looking at him that chances were he had not seen any of our television programs.

How did he know I was a minister? All because I had taken time to talk with him and greet him with such love, he could tell that I was a minister. Even if I had not been a minister as in a preacher, I still would have classified as a minister because I was ministering unto this man. I ministered through kindness; and it just did something to him and it brightened up his whole day and he said, "thank you so much minister."

You may be thinking that after the 40 days, you can just go back to not giving, but Jesus commanded us to do this all of the time. We are supposed to be givers all of the time. We are supposed to be looking for people in need. We are supposed to be a blessing unto the world. We are supposed to be the salt of the earth. People are supposed to look at us and know that we are Christians representing Christ just by the way that we carry ourselves.

I became so friendly with strangers on the program that they thought I wanted some money from them. They just weren't used to it. One guy was so unaccustomed to strangers being nice that he began to cringe when I started talking to him. It was almost as if he wanted to say, "listen brother, I only have a little change and I need this to get me something to eat." I told him that I just wanted to talk to him and that I wanted nothing in return except his conversation. After the initial shock, it totally flipped his outlook toward me. Real kindness is so rare these days that people are afraid to be nice back to you, but we should still try. Just try being nice and don't wait for them to greet you. Go up and begin talking with them and see how it changes their very countenance.

What are the benefits of giving? When we go on a new job, that's usually the second question after we ask about the pay; we want to know about the benefit package. Matthew 19:27 reads, in the NIV, "Peter answered, we have left everything to follow you, what then will there be for us. Jesus said to them, I tell you the truth at the renewal of all things, when the son of man sits down on his glorious throne, you who have followed me will also sit on 12 thrones judging 12 tribes of Israel and everyone who has left houses or brothers or sisters or fathers or mothers or children or fields for my sake will receive 100 times as much and will inherit eternal life. But many who are first will be last and many who are last will be first."

God is guaranteeing the disciples a 100-fold return on their investment of giving for Christ's sake.

People who know me know that I am really into investing and they will often ask me what I recommend that they invest in. What stock, which mutual fund or what other investment? The best and most secure investment that I am confident in is Jesus. I've invested in or studied stocks, mutual funds, options, high yield interest programs, forex, foreclosures, tax liens, bonds, real estate and there's no investment that I know of that will yield the kinds of returns that Jesus promised by giving.

Sure, it's possible to invest your money in the stock market for 30 years and receive 10% a year compounding interest on that money for 30 years. At the end of those 30 years you'll have 17 times whatever you put in. That's pretty good, but it's not great when you think about what Jesus is offering. Not only is Jesus promising 100-fold, but most of you will be too old to really even enjoy that 17-fold that you were not allowed to touch until it matured after the full 30 years. If this life is temporary and Heaven is eternal, wouldn't it be better to invest in eternity than in the "here and now." You have to leave all your 17-fold return here on Earth.

What it boils down to is that Jesus was the best financial planner in all of history. I've read about 30 financial books and no formula in any of the books will produce the kinds of returns that Jesus talked about. Not only does it produce a greater return, it produces a return that will last forever. Giving is not always in money but it always requires giving up something whether it is time, energy, possession, or just sharing something you own.

In all of the financial books that I've read they talk about the time value of money; and three things that determine the amount of money you'll have in the future is the amount that is invested, the interest rate and the length of time that it is in there. With the formula that Jesus gave, the interest rate is 100-fold and the longer the time the more money at the end. The day that you enter heaven will be longer than the last day that you spend on earth. So Jesus' plan has the highest interest rate combined with the longest time span.

Although Jesus is the greatest financial advisor and even though we know and believe His offer and promise, sometimes our vision is still like that of children. The more immature you are the shorter the distance is that you are able to see into the future.

If I ask all of my kids "Would you rather have this bag of candy right now or would you rather own the whole candy store in 20 years from now?" they'd all choose the bag of candy now.

If I asked them "Would you rather get a season pass to Six Flags Amusement Park and we go once a week over the summer or would you rather own Six Flags in 20 years?" they would all choose the season pass.

If I asked them "Would you rather have an X-box right now with all of the games in the store or would you rather own Microsoft in 20 years?" even though it's billions of dollars, they'd say give me the games and the X-box right now.

That's childish vision. They can't see the future. God asks us for just a measly 10% and we'd rather keep the 10% versus having the favor of God over our finances.

Getting on this program will definitely change your heart and make you more giving. Everybody's looking for a blessing but few want to become a blessing. Jesus said that it's more blessed to give than it is to receive. This may sound deep at first, but just think back on the last few people who have asked you for something. Now ask yourself which situation would you rather have been in: the person asking or the person giving. That simplifies that whole statement. I tell you that your miracle awaits you at the end of your 40 days.

Before you go to the next chapter, I'll leave you with this. My mother is a prime example of a giving and generous spirit. I don't think she has a greedy bone in her body. She's clothed and fed and helped people and underprivileged kids her entire life.

People have always talked about seeing angels here on earth with supernatural means, but if you've seen my mother, you've seen an angel here on earth. In most of the paintings or pictures that we see, the angels are always painted with halos over their heads. I remember Mama taking a picture with other people sitting around a table. Nothing miraculous happened when the photographer took the picture, but once it was developed, you could see as clear as day a halo of light around my mother's head. She wasn't the only person in the picture, but she was the only one in the picture with the glow of light. My mother is living proof that God desires that we be angels here on Earth.

You may be the only angel that some people will meet. You will be the only representative of Christ that they will ever see.

One day the pastor and I were looking at the account online for MountainWings.com and there was an error there. Instead of a few thousand dollars, it said that the balance on the MountainWings account was 55 trillion dollars. He checked it and ran a report and it kept saying the same thing: 55 trillion dollars. He told me about it and I looked at it all kinds of ways. It said the same thing: 55 trillion dollars. He prayed about it and asked about the significance of it and God told him that the figure is an accurate balance for his Heavenly bank account.

The pastor wrote a story about that experience. Just go to AirJesus.com and click "Past Issues" and put "trillion" in the search box and read about it.

There's no investment here on Earth that can yield that kind of return. The more we understand, the more we can see why Jesus wants us to store up treasures in Heaven where the canker worm cannot get to it and the moth can't eat it up.

It's Me!

There's an old song that we used to sing in church and the words simply say "the more you give, He gives to you; just keep on giving, because it's really true that you can't beat God's giving." That's amazing and so awesome. We just learned that we can combat greed with generosity and no matter how much we give in time or in blessings, we can't out-give God.

He will ALWAYS return what we invested in Him and then some. But I will tell you this, from personal experience, you can have more than enough financially to give to others once you choose to be obedient to God. You must learn to give your 10% and an offering as God has instructed us to do. Why would God bless you with more if you haven't been faithful over what He's already given? Be a good steward over what you already have and greed will go away.

Proclamation for Greed

Number Six: I pledge that I will give someone something material each day. The size does not matter. Whether it is a dollar or a donut or buying someone's lunch, I must give someone "other than my own children" something each day. At least every other day it must be someone OUTSIDE of my family. If I am a member of a church, during this period I will give to my church as directed by my church. Concentrating on giving helps me to control greed and realize my own blessings.

Chapter Eight

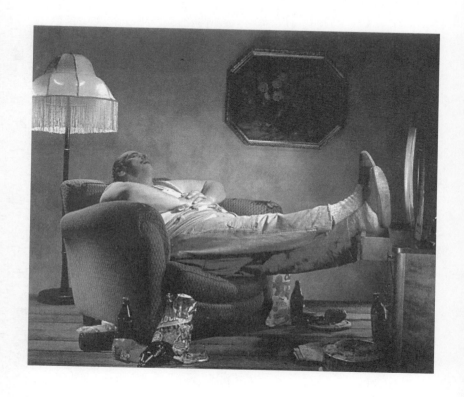

Sloth: Busy Being Lazy

By C. Elijah Bronner

What is sloth? II Thessalonians 3:6-12, Contemporary English Version, reads, "And now dear brothers and sisters, we give you this command with the authority of our Lord Jesus Christ, stay away from any Christian who lives in idleness and doesn't follow the traditions of hard work we gave you. For you know that you ought to follow our example. We were never lazy when we were with you. We never accepted food from anyone without paying for it. We worked hard day and night so that we would not be a burden to any of you. It wasn't that we did not have the right to ask you to feed us, but we wanted to give you an example to follow. Even while we were with you, we gave you this rule: whoever does not work should not eat. Yet we hear that some of you are living idle lives refusing to work and wasting time meddling in other people's business. In the name of the Lord Jesus Christ we appeal to such people and command them to settle down and get to work."

Even the King James Version of II Thessalonians 3:6-12 confirms that the Thessalonians were busy bodies, but they weren't working at anything. They were busy being lazy. Read the verses again. We know that there is power in the name of Jesus, but I've never heard the name of Jesus used like this. We call on Him to raise the dead and to heal the sick and to cast out demons, but never to command laziness to leave someone. He was commanding the spirit of laziness to leave in the name of Jesus.

Being lazy is a real problem. We are all lazy at different times and in different ways. Sometimes it's a spirit that just comes over you and by the time you realize it, you can't really get rid of it. A man once told me that he went through a period in his life where everything about him was slothful. He was inexplicably lethargic. He just lay in the bed until noon everyday. He had jobs that he would quit for no reason. He had a chair in the living room and he would just sit there for hours at a time doing nothing - just sitting there looking at the wall. He didn't cut the grass; he didn't do anything around the house. This spirit had such a hold on him so he began to pray about it. It took a year, but God finally delivered him from that spirit of laziness.

God intends for us to have meaningful work and to use what He has given us. The man I just spoke of repented for being lazy and vowed to God that he would be diligent. He began confessing and proclaiming that he would be a diligent man everyday in everything he did. But one day while he was working in the garage, he got frustrated and gave up. Just as he walked off, the Lord spoke to him and quickly reminded him of his promise to be diligent. The Lord told him that a diligent man doesn't quit. If you start something, you should finish it. He repented and went back into that garage and finished the project. He was rewarded with an overwhelming sense of accomplishment.

Something else happened in II Thessalonians; the people got saved. It was good that they got saved, but when they got saved, they quit working. They were convinced that Jesus was on His way back soon so they just quit working. They just sat around singing hymns waiting on Jesus to return. The apostle Paul addressed them and let them know that they needed to get to work.

Sometimes we have the idea that when we get saved we can just take it easy and that we don't have to work any longer, and we can just wait on Jesus to come back. But in II Thessalonians 4:11, we are instructed to work hard so that those who don't know Christ will respect us. In other words, don't worry about trying to witness to your boss on the job. Paul said work hard and your hard work will speak for you. Even people who don't know Christ will respect you for the work that you do. He said let your work be a witness to Christ. Hard work represents Jesus Christ but it is a shame that we have allowed laziness to represent Christ.

Pastor Nathaniel doesn't even hire people who come in heavily talking about Jesus because his experience has shown that they are not going to work as diligently as he would like them to. Do your job, get there on time, and work harder than anybody else; then your boss is going to pull you to the side and ask what is it that's causing you to go beyond the call of duty. What is this spirit of excellence? Why are you working so hard for me when everyone else is goofing off? I haven't given you a raise. I haven't honored you. Why are you pouring yourself out in such an exemplary manner? When you are noticed to this extent, you then have permission to let him know about Jesus.

Paul said to take hard work and use it as a witnessing tool. Get busy at your job, be the best worker at your company. Be known for hard work and for fervency and for being effective and getting the job done. When your company needs something done your name should be at the top of the list. There is an old saying that we shouldn't be "so Heavenly-minded that we're no Earthly good."

Sharing Jesus when you are supposed to be working will lead to slothfulness because you will find yourself socializing more than working. Christians have given such a bad light to Christ. Christians should have a lower unemployment rate than anybody. We should be the hardest working people in the world, not necessarily in the number of hours that we work, but in the quality and quantity of our work.

Where does the word "sloth" come from? Did you know that a "sloth" is an animal? Pastor Nathaniel has traveled to the

Rain Forest and has seen some living in trees. Although the sloth is the size of a large house cat, it is the slowest moving animal on Earth. If you put a sloth on the ground, it would take him one month to walk one kilometer. That's not just slow; that's real slow. I don't necessarily blame the sloth for going so slow. Their choice of speed has a purpose. They move slowly because it is part of their defense mechanisms against predators.

A lot of predators can't see very well but they can sense motion. When they sense motion they can launch on their prey. Therefore God gave them the knowledge to move slowly as part of their survival. That's their protection system.

Why do you move slowly on projects and tasks? What are you protecting yourself from? Work? If you put a sloth in front of a motion detector, the alarm would never go off. I know some of you women are thinking that you married a sloth and you wish he would go get in a tree, anything to get him off the couch. Just remember, it may take him a month.

Not only does the sloth move very slowly, but he sleeps a lot too. As a matter of fact, the average sloth sleeps 15 hours a day. They live most of their lives hanging upside down on the tree limbs, sleeping. Hmm…a sloth spends his day moving slowly and sleeping. Anybody you know? So that's how we get the word "lazy" from "sloth." The word "sloth" comes from the animal and means slow, sluggish and lazy.

I remember reading that one man remarked, "it may be true that hard work never killed anybody, but I figured why take the chance?" Jimmy Lyons said, "Tomorrow is the only day of the year that appeals to a lazy man." Henry Clay said, "That the time will come when winter would even ask you what you were doing all summer."

We're all lazy in some shape, form or fashion, at some time

or another. If you think about it, all of the major inventions that we have or have had were invented because we were lazy and wanted to find an easy way to do things that required less work.

People got tired of walking so they invented the automobile. We get real creative when we get lazy. We start thinking of ways to do things faster and easier. Think about it. Somebody got tired of hand washing the dishes and clothes so they invented the dishwasher and the washing machine.

Back in the old days people were very active. They scrubbed clothes on the washboard and they got out in the back yard and cut firewood. Now we can just go to the store, buy a Duraflame®, throw it on the fireplace and light a match to it.

As a result of doing less, we are getting sicker. So we lost a lot of our activity and as a result we're getting sicker because we're not exercising. We're no longer doing our daily chores like we used to before these fancy inventions. All of these things were invented to make things more convenient and to put you more at ease; to make us lazy.

God says that we should be careful so that we don't allow that spirit to corrupt us. Sloth is literally spiritual laziness. Sloth does not necessarily mean that you are lying around doing nothing at all. Sloth also means that you're not doing the things that you should be doing. You are doing things that serve no purpose. That's what sloth is from a spiritual standpoint. You're busy but you're idle.

Busyness connected with sloth is an enemy to the things of God. You use your busyness as an excuse not to pray. We're so busy that we use it as an excuse, but if you don't have time for God, that's being slothful. We say, "I'm busy, I don't have time to read my Bible. I'm just busy." No, in God's eyes, you're slothful even though there is a lot of activity.

Paul says that you're spiritually lazy and entering into the realm of sloth. Lazy people always make excuses. A wife asked her husband when was he going to fix the roof. He said, "When it's raining I can't fix it, and when it's not raining it doesn't need fixing." You can't argue with lazy people; they have very good excuses.

The Bible says it takes seven men of wisdom to handle one lazy man. A lazy man is clever. He makes up logical reasons for not doing something. Stop the excuses. Stop being lazy. Stop being slothful. Be fervent and diligent in the things of God.

The 40 Day Miracle requires a daily, regimented schedule of reading your Bible and praying. This is a great way to fight off sloth. The formula for how long you should spend time reading and praying is very simple. You should read your Bible and pray for the number of minutes that equal your age.

If you're 40 years old then you need 40 minutes total of Scripture reading and prayer each day. You can pray for 10 minutes in the morning and then read your Bible for 10 minutes in the morning. At this point half of your work is done. Before you go to bed you pray another 10 minutes and read your Bible another 10 minutes. That's 40 minutes for that day.

Once you do the calculation (take your age and you divide it by 4), if you come up with a fraction, round it up to the next whole number. If you come up to where your calculations equal 9 ½ minutes because of your age just round it up to 10 minutes. Don't be too lazy to throw in an extra 30 seconds. When you start spending time with God then you'll realize after a while that it's no longer a chore.

Another way to battle laziness is to be eager to do something. Eagerness battles laziness and it will lead you to enjoying the very thing you were too lazy to do in the beginning.

You'll start looking forward to it. When you are really enjoying something, the time goes by. You'll find yourself going over your time. It's like when you're in love and you call your girlfriend or your boyfriend, you don't have to sit there and look down at your watch to make sure you talk to them at least 15 minutes. The hours fly by. So when you start enjoying your time and your fellowship in prayer and in reading the word it will counteract spiritual laziness known as sloth.

So when God drops it in your heart to do something, you'll do it because you're no longer lazy. So don't get caught up in being so busy. If you're too busy to spend time with God every day, you are too busy. You will notice that your life will begin to change once you begin to make that daily commitment - your age in minutes twice a day. Do this on a daily basis and you're going to find sloth dissipating out of your life.

I once saw a commercial for a product called Electro Sol® for the dishwasher. I don't know if you can get any lazier than Electro Sol. The commercial demonstrated that when you get ready to put the dishes in the dishwasher, you don't even have to scrape the plates; you just stick them in there full of food.

Of course I wanted to get a bottle, especially since it eliminated the chore of having to scrape plates. Notice, the world is always trying to make it more convenient for you so that you have to do less and less work.

The Bible says that poverty will come to a lazy man like an armed robber. Poverty will rip you off when you're lazy. The Bible says that a lazy man is the brother to a destroyer, and I realize that it's because laziness destroys your life. It destroys your potential, your gifts and your talents. It destroys your dreams. It literally makes your life a wasteland.

In Proverbs, one man said that he went by the field of a lazy man and it taught him a lesson in life. He said when he looked at the lazy man's field, he had neglected it so much by refusing to work it that it looked the same as if a destroyer had come by and destroyed it.

There's no difference between a destroyer and a lazy man. If you have a beautiful field and somebody came by and set it on fire and destroyed it that is no different than a lazy man who lies there idly not tending to the field. All of the advantages and opportunities were missed. All of the produce that could have come out of that field never came out. Everything that could happen in your life will never happen if you are lazy. It is like a barren field with broken down walls and a lazy man just looking at all of it. A lazy man is the brother to a destroyer. Laziness will destroy your life.

The Bible says one man is so lazy that when he's eating he puts his hand into the plate and he's so lazy that he won't even return his hand to his mouth. That's lazy. The Bible says that as a door turns on it's hinges so does a lazy man turn over in the bed. Laziness. Poverty comes to lazy people. Prosperity comes to those who are diligent. A lazy man always wishes for something but the Bible says he will never get it. He only wishes. It's the man who will get up and do something who will have something in life.

It's Me!

Sloth is tricky because it's so comfortable and relaxing. Inventions make life easier and we don't really have to do a lot of work. Most people can not afford to lie around the house all day watching television so most people do not suffer from laziness or slothfulness as we normally think of it. Instead, because most people do lack in financial stability, they tend to work so much that they allow their busyness to be their excuse for sleeping in on Sunday or not being able to make it to Bible Study. If slothfulness will prevent you from prosperity then you may want to consider putting God first and being diligent in your spiritual life.

Proclamation for Sloth

Number Seven: I will pray and read scripture for my age in minutes daily.**

Each morning I will pray for ___ minutes and read scripture for ___ minutes. Before bed I will pray for ____ minutes and read scripture for ____ minutes. This helps me to control spiritual laziness and to know the Word and Voice of God.

Chapter Nine

Connect the Dots

You did it! You defeated sloth long enough to make it to the end of the book. Now that you have finished the book, do you see the correlation? All seven sins are connected in some way or another and when you begin to conquer one, the others fall in line. Remember, you have to have 3D Vision to succeed in the program. You must discover, decide and do. Even to "do," you have to overcome the spirit of laziness or sloth.

To overcome **sloth**, you have to let go of your **pride** and admit that you do have a problem with at least one if not all of the seven sins. When you let go of your pride, you will be able to see that you need this program and you will do it. In letting go of the spirit of laziness, you will see prosperity in your diligence. We learned that poverty only comes when we are lazy. When God is blessing you, you will be grateful for the things you have and you will "want what you have," eliminating **envy** from your life. In eliminating envy, you will begin to look in your own closet and see the blessings of God without being **greedy** for more. If you no longer want more than what you already have, then you will no longer want someone else's husband or wife, boyfriend or girlfriend or the sexual trickery of the devil. You will be fighting against **lust**. Since we lust after more than just sex, you will also be fighting the lust of eating until you're full: **gluttony**. Since we often overeat because our emotions are out of control; and if we can learn to pull away from the plate no matter what, we will be able to handle all of our emotional issues, including **anger** a lot better.

I don't know which sin you will have the most difficult time with, but once you discover what it is and decide that you are going to do this, you will be blessed. You will receive a new life, a new spirit and a new outlook on other people. We can't encourage you enough by letting you know this Miracle will change your life for the better. Please visit 40day.com for more information, helpful tools, FAQs and for any of the sermons in their entirety. Testimonies from people who are already on the program have been coming in and these people are losing weight and being blessed with cars and financial blessings and breakthroughs. All types of things are already beginning to happen and now it's your turn. So if at first you don't succeed, start over! We all do. The important thing is that you do it until you succeed! May God bless you before, during and after your 40 Day Miracle.

**And the LORD answered me,
and said,**
Write the vision,
*and make it plain upon tables,
that he may run that readeth it.*
(Hab 2:2 KJV)

Write Day Number beside each entry:

_____

_____

_____

_____

_____

_____

_____

_____

_____

_____

_____

_____

_____

_____

_____

_____

_____

_____

_____

_____

_____

_____

_____

_____

_____

_____

_____

_____

_____

_____

_____

_____

_____

_____

Journal

Journal

Frequently Asked Questions

Q: I'd like to wait a while before I start, is that OK?
A: You need to listen to a particular message in the "Conquering the Nations" series called "ProcrastiNATION" at AirJesus.com. The sooner you start The 40 Day Miracle, the better.

Q: Is there a support group to help me?
A: There is a forum and testimony section at 40day.com. You can sign-up free and participate. It is completely optional. Most who do The 40 Day Miracle don't sign up, less than 5% do. When you write and share the vision, it helps to solidify your commitment and to help encourage others as they read about your experiences.

Q: Can I listen to Scripture on audio Bibles instead of reading?
A: Yes, we have the full spoken Bible and the Bible to read online at AirJesus.com. Both are FREE.

Q: What if I mess up before the 40 days are over?
A: Violations are most likely to occur within the first few days. The longer we are on the program, the less likely we are to slip up. Slip ups fall into two categories: unintentional slips and deliberate pre-planned slip ups. If you slip up and it is deliberately pre-planned, then you must start over. God has granted you far more than just one 40-day period so if you slip up and you knew in advance that you were going to violate (for example fornication or a premeditated argument), just start over. It is spiritually imperative that you complete the full 40 days without deliberate deviation. To hear how the pastor failed several times yet triumphed during his 40-day breakthrough, read the chapter again, LUST-Gotta Have It.

If it is an unintentional slip up, then you must immediately counteract it with DOUBLE the reverse of the slip up. If you complain about something, then you must IMMEDIATELY counteract the negative complaint with two positive statements about the situation. For example, if traffic has been stuck for 30 minutes and you complain saying, "This traffic has been stuck for 30 minutes," you must immediately counteract the negative complaint. You could say, "but my air-condition is working good," or "at least I don't have to use the bathroom" or "I have plenty of gas in the tank."

If you get angry and raise your voice you must immediately counteract it with TWO positive statements or emotions. For example a BIG smile or an "I love you so much!" statement.

If you eat until you are full then you must SKIP TWO MEALS that you would normally eat. If you don't normally eat breakfast or lunch, then skipping those would not count.

If you miss your prayer time or scripture reading then you must pray or read double to make up for the missed item. For example, if you are supposed to read and pray ten minutes each and you miss either morning or evening, then you would need to pray and read an additional twenty minutes (double time) for the missed item.

Remember, the time spent on The 40 Day Miracle is NOT negative. We should strive to live this way each day so if we are on it longer then it is beneficial, not negative.

Q: Do I need to listen to the 7 messages or read the book before I start?
A: No, but you need to listen to at least one per day or read one chapter per day once you start. That will allow you to finish listening or reading the first time in one week. You must listen to or read the 7 messages at least twice during the 40 days. You need the

messages to help you fully understand what you are doing and to give you guidance on how to do each one.

Q: Does The Fullness Anointing wear off?
A: If it does, simply listen again to the complete message.

Q: Can I read other Christian material other than scripture?
A: Yes, but you MUST read your allotted minutes of scripture. If you want to read other material in addition, then that's great.

Q: Suppose I want to add something else during my 40 days?
A: Fine, just don't remove anything. If there is something else in particular that you struggle with, then by all means include it also and add it to the Daily Proclamation.

Q: Do I need to read ALL of the Daily Proclamation each time or can I just read the bold print portion.
A: Read ALL of it for the first seven days. You can read just the BOLD print after seven days if you choose.

Q: I don't think I can make it 40 days, can I do it less days?
A: You CAN make it 40 days. Don't lessen what God has for you. It was not easy for anyone in the Bible either, but God strengthened them as He will strengthen you. The 40 Day journey was a specific number. It took Elijah 40 days to reach Mt. Horeb and hear God. If he had only traveled 39 days he would have never made it. Don't even think about getting less than the full 40-Day Miracle God has in store for you.

Q: I don't go to church regularly or at all, can I still participate in The 40 Day Miracle?
A: Most who are in and out of the church have major issues. "Oh God, have mercy on me a sinner," is one of the greatest prayers ever prayed. Complete The 40 Day Miracle and watch God work the miracle in your life.

Q: Suppose I do this and nothing happens?
A: Are you kidding? Just no anger or complaining for 40 days will change your world. If you follow The 40 Day Miracle, something great WILL happen.

Q: I'm too much of a wreck to improve.
A: If you are not dead, you're not too much of a wreck. How many Christians have you murdered? Well, that's what Paul was doing and he ended up writing more in the New Testament than anyone else. God specializes in taking a mess and making a miracle.

Q: How do I know if this is for me?
A: Take a look at the 7 Things The 40 Day Miracle addresses. If you have one or more of the 7 issues, then it's for you.

Q: Do I need to do this alone or can I ask others to join me?
A: One can put a thousand to flight but two can put ten thousand to flight. (Deu. 32:30) It is why Jesus sent the disciples out in pairs. When someone does The 40 Day Miracle with you, both of you will strengthen and help the other. If no one can see the vision and join you, don't let that stop you. The more that you get to participate, the greater the glory and the miracle. Try to get as large a group as possible to experience The 40 Day Miracle with you.

Q: Why do I need the 7 messages and why read or listen twice?
A: We considered having an alternative message that summed up the seven but God spoke and said, "Anyone who will not be diligent enough to listen to the seven messages would not be diligent enough to complete The 40 Day Miracle." Therefore we did not make a summary message. You MUST listen to or read all seven messages. You simply must have the spiritual and practical background on what you are doing and why you are doing it. Changes will start when you begin to listen and read.

When you listen or read the second time, you will receive things that you missed the first time. The longer you are on The 40 Day Miracle, the more meaning each message has to you each time you hear it.

Q: How and why do I need to "round up" the number of minutes that I read scripture and pray if it is a partial minute? If I am 25 years old, can't I just pray for 6.25 minutes each time instead of 7 minutes?
A: Rounding up will add either 15, 30, or 45 seconds per session. Even minutes keep it simple especially if you use a full minute timer. The positive side is that you could get up to an extra 45 seconds of scripture reading and prayer than someone whose age divides out evenly. The 40 Day Miracle trains our spirits to focus on the positives of life.

As we are asked and answer new pertinent questions, we will put them in the FAQ section on The40DayMiracle.com. Reading the FAQs reinforces certain points and will make sure you are kept informed of any changes.

AGE/MINUTES CALCULATIONS

You are to read scripture and pray for your age in minutes daily. The time is divided evenly between scripture reading and prayer, and between morning and before bed each day.

For example, if you are 20 years old, you must read scripture for five minutes in the morning, pray for five minutes in the morning, read scripture for five minutes before bed and pray for five minutes before bed. The total time of scripture reading and prayer per day will be equal to or slightly greater than your age.

Partial minutes will be rounded up to the next minute.
Below is the age/minute table. The first number is the age and the second number gives the minutes for reading and prayer per session. The minutes number is the number that you will use to fill-in the blanks on the Daily Proclamation.

Age/Minutes
Use the minutes number to fill-in the blanks on the
Daily Proclamation

10/3 11/3 12/3 13/4 14/4 15/4 16/4 17/5 18/5 19/5 20/5
21/6 22/6 23/6 24/6 25/7 26/7 27/7 28/7 29/8 30/8 31/8
32/8 33/9 34/9 35/9 36/9 37/10 38/10 39/10 40/10 41/11
42/11 43/11 44/11 45/12 46/12 47/12 48/12 49/13 50/13
51/13 52/13 53/14 54/14 55/14 56/14 57/15 58/15 59/15
60/15 61/16 62/16 63/16 64/16 65/17 66/17 67/17 68/17
69/18 70/18 71/18 72/18 73/19 74/19 75/19 76/19 77/20
78/20 79/20 80/20 81/21 82/21 83/21 84/21 85/22 86/22
87/22 88/22 89/23 90/23 91/23 91/23 92/23 93/24 94/24
95/24 96/24 97/25 98/25

THE 40 DAY MIRACLE DAILY PROCLAMATION

Dear God I surrender my life to you. Help me to change my will to Thy will.

I will listen to the seven messages or read this book twice *giving me the Scriptural and practical basis for each of the seven areas of The 40 Day Miracle. Just as your Son was tempted for a 40 day period, just as Moses had two 40 day experiences on the mountain, just as Elijah fasted during a 40 day journey to hear God, just as You opened the windows of heaven and cleansed the earth during a 40 day rain, and just as Jesus appeared during a 40 day span after His resurrection,* **I consecrate before You this 40 day season for my change.**

I ask for and expect to be a new creature after this 40 day consecration. I ask for and expect The 40 Day Miracle within my life, mind, and spirit. Opposition, resistance, and challenge will come; but I know that greater is He who is within me than he who is in the world. I will overcome every temptation, opposition,

doubter, resistance, challenge, and past habit.
With your help Dear God, I will succeed.

During this 40 day period for The 40 Day Miracle
I , _____ ,
pledge the following:

**Number One: I pledge to read this statement
aloud each morning and night** *and it will take root
within my heart. This helps to reduce my pride and
helps me to realize that I can do all things through
Christ who strengthens me and that I can do
nothing successfully without you O God.*

**Number Two: I pledge that I will compliment
someone each day and will say nothing
negative about anyone.** *Each day I will find and
tell someone something good or great about
themselves. I cannot count the compliments of the
same person more than twice within any one week
towards this pledge. I will not gossip or make
negative statements of any kind about another
person. This combats envy as it focuses me on
others and gears me to be happy for them instead
of focusing on myself.*

Number Three: I pledge that I will stop eating BEFORE I am full. *Health experts and medical research have long confirmed that we live longer and are healthier if we stop eating before we are full; therefore, I will leave the table still slightly hungry. This helps me to control the flesh's strongest physical craving which is food, and helps me to control gluttony. If I have a tendency to overeat, I will listen once per week to message #3 – Gluttony, at 40day.com or on CD or tape and freely receive The Fullness Anointing at the end of the message. I WILL stop eating at each meal BEFORE I am full.*

Number Four: If I am doing this, *I pledge that I will stop flirting, having affairs, committing fornication, looking at pornography, or communicating with a person who is not my spouse or who is an ex. This helps to control the lust within me.*

Number Five: I pledge that I will not get angry, curse or complain. *I will not raise my voice in anger. Nothing great or small will make me angry or react in anger. I will not complain about ANYTHING. Not the weather, not the government, not the news, not my aches, not my money, not my kids, my spouse, my job, my car, traffic, or anything else.* **I will NOT complain about ANYTHING!**

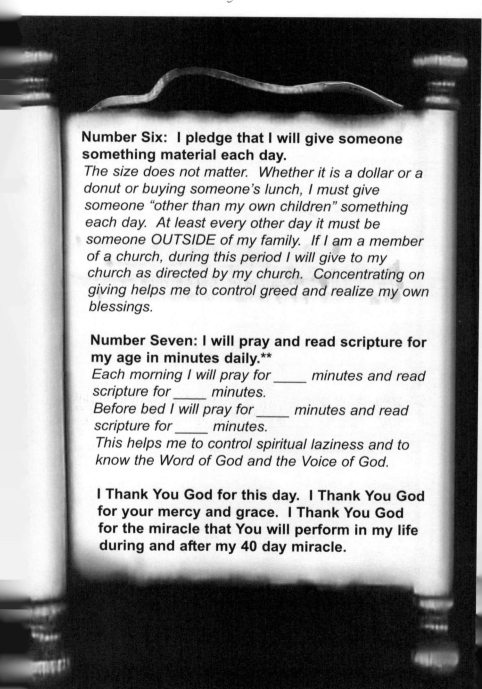

Number Six: I pledge that I will give someone something material each day.

The size does not matter. Whether it is a dollar or a donut or buying someone's lunch, I must give someone "other than my own children" something each day. At least every other day it must be someone OUTSIDE of my family. If I am a member of a church, during this period I will give to my church as directed by my church. Concentrating on giving helps me to control greed and realize my own blessings.

Number Seven: I will pray and read scripture for my age in minutes daily.**

Each morning I will pray for _____ minutes and read scripture for _____ minutes.
Before bed I will pray for _____ minutes and read scripture for _____ minutes.
This helps me to control spiritual laziness and to know the Word of God and the Voice of God.

I Thank You God for this day. I Thank You God for your mercy and grace. I Thank You God for the miracle that You will perform in my life during and after my 40 day miracle.

Congratulations

Prepare
to receive

Your Miracle!

...It is finished.